100+ Winning Answers to the Toughest Interview Questions

Second Edition

Casey Hawley, M.A.

BARRON'S

DEDICATION

To all the people who have championed me in my career so faithfully all these years. George Haynes, Kathy Harber, Ron Hart, Brenda Call, Ellery Queen, Emma Henry, Mardette Coleman, John Steed, Bob Thomas, Susan Wise, Barbara Pagano, Rita DeBow, Sharon Smith, Sharon Powell, Randy Stone, and many others who helped me secure interviews and succeed in the interviewing process. Your professionalism is exceeded only by your generosity. God bless you.

All inquiries should be addressed to:
Barron's Educational Series, Inc.
250 Wireless Boulevard
Hauppauge, NY 11788
www.barronseduc.com

Library of Congress Catalog Card No. 2007052953

ISBN-13: 978-0-7641-3912-3
ISBN-10: 0-7641-3912-6

Library of Congress Cataloging-in-Publication Data
Hawley, Casey Fitts.
    100+ winning answers to the toughest interview questions / Casey Hawley.
— 2nd ed.
        p.   cm.—(Business success guide)
    Includes index.
    ISBN-13: 978-0-7641-3912-3
    ISBN-10: 0-7641-3912-6

    1. Employment interviewing. I. Title. II. Title: One hundred plus winning answers to the toughest interview questions.

    HF5549.5.I6H38   2008
    650.14'4—dc22   2007052953

PRINTED IN CHINA
9 8 7 6 5 4 3 2

Contents

◆

Introduction

◆

100+ Winning Answers to the Toughest Interview Questions gives the instant answers the serious job seeker is looking for in preparation for a job interview. Why are these answers a cut above the more than 1,000 books out there on interview questions?

◆ This is a serious and well-thought-out approach to answering questions.

◆ The answers have been carefully refined and phrased to project confidence.

◆ The tone of the language is positive and upbeat. Managers and supervisors doing interviews respond especially well to this.

◆ The answers are easy to remember with the addition of some helpful tips in the book.

◆ The questions and answers are realistic.

In my work as a corporate consultant, I conduct a popular seminar titled "Career Change Management." I recently realized that my corporate clients and the attendees at my career seminars have been requesting a book like this for years. The question I have been asked hundreds of times is, "Do you know of a book of just questions for interviews?" I see my seminar attendees pick up their notebooks in the mornings and flip through to find the interview

questions. This timely book has those great questions every interviewee can anticipate, and then furnishes the pefect answers.

WHAT EVERY INTERVIEW QUESTION BOOK
SHOULD HAVE, PLUS MUCH MORE

Every interview question book should cover the most frequently
asked questions, and this one does. Every interview book should
offer some pat, easy answers for novice job seekers, and this one
does. If a book addresses only traditional questions and pat
answers, however, two very important factors will be overlooked:

1. Professional interviewers are often turned off by pat answers.
   The applicant's sincerity, possibly even veracity, is questioned.

2. Studies by Xerox, Yale, and others show that the delivery of the answer is more important than the content of the answer. *100+ Winning Answers to the Toughest Interview Questions* equips the reader to triumph over both of these hurdles.

First, the pat answers are enhanced by a host of fill-in-the-blank, flexible answers to fit almost any interview situation. These easily customized answers show job candidates how to adapt their answers to

◆ sound fresh, authentic, and unrehearsed.

◆ reflect their personality and unique style.

◆ distinguish them from the field and create a favorable and lasting impression.

Chapter 1

The Perfect
Answer Is
Triple-A Rated

◆

*There are two kinds of people in the world—
those who walk into a room and say, "There
you are" and those who say, "Here I am!"*
—Abigail Van Buren

The perfect answer is Triple-A Rated:

◆ Authentic

◆ Automatic

◆ Accurate

When someone interviews you for that all-important job, you must sound as if you mean what you say. It has become a common practice to exaggerate and even lie in job interviews or on résumés. Here's how to set yourself apart from the pack with Triple-A-Rated answers:

◆ *Authentic.* Does the answer ring true? Can the applicant be viewed as sincere when giving this answer or does the answer sound canned? Interviewers know that all applicants will profess to be experienced, hardworking, reliable, and creative. To convince an interviewer, most applicants will say almost anything to prove they are the best suited for the available jobs. How do interviewers decide which applicants are telling the truth and which are creating a rosy but false picture? Interviewers tell us that textbook answers are a clue that the applicant may not be authentic. Pat, patronizing answers are a turnoff widely professed by job interviewers. The techniques in this book teach job seekers how to answer with great sincerity. The flexibility of the answers helps avoid the tone that the applicant is parroting answers from a book.

◆ *Automatic.* Answers must be so easy to remember that they come to mind easily. Very complex and wildly creative answers may sound great in a book, but will a reader remember them weeks later? Remember, these answers must jump to mind when the reader is under great stress. Easy, clear, forthright answers sell an applicant's skills and personality best.

◆ *Accurate.* Interviewers want exactly the information they ask for—and not a sentence more. Answering questions, especially sensitive ones, with clarity and succinctness wins points. Readers are encouraged to prepare answers with a few dates, examples, and mini case studies from their actual experience. This boosts credibility, a key factor in being the candidate chosen for the job.

Chapter 2

---◆---

The S.S.S. Method for Fast and Fantastic Answers

◆

Talk low, talk slow, and don't say too much.
—John Wayne

You are sitting in the hot seat—the interview chair. The interviewer pops a tough question. How do you quickly respond with a winning answer?

Answers that win jobs are *specific*, *short*, and *supportive*. If you can, make every answer fit these criteria. You will be the most credible candidate for the job.

TIPS FOR APPLYING S.S.S.

SPECIFIC

The best answers are factually specific and even measurable. Here are just a few specifics that interviewers love:

Dollar Amounts

◆ "The total budget I managed was more than $300,000."

◆ "I saved the company $2,000 monthly on insurance costs."

◆ "I managed a department of 300 employees."

Percentages

◆ "A 10 percent reduction of rework resulted from the quality control measures I implemented."

◆ "I cut production costs by 8 percent the first year."

◆ "We were able to process claims 15 percent faster after I reorganized the department."

◆ "Absenteeism dropped 8 percent after I became manager."

Industry Measures

◆ "My department increased our service capacity by 9 megawatts without adding any additional staff."

◆ "Based on my recommendation, we were successfully able to treat each batch of cross ties with 2.5 gallons of the chemicals instead of the full 3.0. The same high standards of durability have been maintained, yet the savings add up considerably over a year's time."

◆ "Since installing the equipment I requested in my business plan, the bank finds that tellers do an average of 20 additional transactions a day."

SHORT

Answer the question with a specific answer but don't elaborate on the background information. Interviewers are usually going through a list of questions. Give a great specific answer, then pause to allow the interviewer to take control of the conversation again.

This is probably the downfall of most experienced people. Interviewees often give good initial answers; unfortunately, they keep talking. As they talk, they divulge more things that could raise red flags to interviewers. After you've given an answer, stop talking! You may talk yourself right out of a job.

SUPPORTIVE

Be sure that your answer sounds positive, warm, and supportive, even if it is businesslike. People hire people they want to be around. Keep in mind that a boss may be coupled with an employee for years. People hire people they wouldn't mind going to lunch with, meeting, and working with as a team. Specifically, drop comments that sound supportive such as the following into the conversation:

◆ Your current boss—"My boss has always supported my ongoing development. He has greatly developed my technical skills."

◆ Your teammates—Give credit to your team for any accomplishment. If asked how you became the top-selling rep in your company, say, "My teammates offered lots of support. Everyone from Market Research to secretaries to my boss deserves part of the credit for that award."

◆ The interviewer—Be very supportive of the interviewer. If he leads you into a conference room, watch for clues about when to sit down or where to sit. If he is interrupted by his secretary and apologizes, be sure to say out loud, "That's perfectly all right. Work goes on."

If he expresses any complaints about his day, his schedule, or anything, be empathetic. Pick up on clues about what is going on with him. Weave those into the conversation to show that you really listened to him.

- "I know these interviews must be cutting into your schedule of year-end audits."

- "It sounds as if Huxley will be difficult to replace. You must be covering some of his duties for him."

WHAT IF THE INTERVIEWER ASKS ABOUT A WEAKNESS?

S.S.S. applies perfectly when the interviewer detects vulnerabilities.

Crisp, direct answers are a must, even when the question has honed in on one of your areas of weakness. Here is one example.

What does one do when the question is, "Tell me about your retail experience," and you know you have less experience than the rest of the group of applicants? What if you have worked only two summer vacations in retail? The temptation is to be vague when confronted with areas of weakness. Hedging can lose the job for you. Instead, tell the truth, but tell it in a way that points up your strengths. Accurate but good answers could include:

◆ "Two companies contributed to my experience in retail." (This is a good answer because it uses a *specific number*. Remember, interviewers *love* specifics. Although you have a total of only six months experience between the two companies, the answer capitalizes on the positives: experience from two diverse companies. Again, you sound supportive of your former employer, a good sign to those doing the interview.)

◆ "The most valuable experience I gained in retail was from Macy's, although The Sharper Image is my more recent experience." (Then go on to elaborate specifically about all the great things you learned at Macy's: inventory, scheduling, customer service. You can make a little experience sound like a lot—plus, you will sound so positive that people will want to hire you!)

◆ "The two most valuable things I have learned from my retail experience are _____ and _____. From Macy's I learned _____. From The Sharper Image I learned _____." (Again, this gives the *specific number*, two, and mentions two *specific companies*. The answers don't sound hesitant or wishy-washy about the interviewee's lack of experience. Even more important, the interviewee doesn't sound apologetic. In the interview, an apologetic tone marks a person as a loser.)

◆ "What I think is most valuable about my experience is the diversity. You couldn't find two more diverse approaches to retail than Macy's and The Sharper Image. I learned all I could at both. Macy's taught me things I could never have learned at The Sharper Image, and vice versa. For example, _____." (Again, the specific number two is used to give a confident, precise answer.)

The next time an interviewer asks a question, think S.S.S. You'll ace the interview with your *specific, short, supportive* responses.

Chapter 3

The Trickiest,
Stickiest Questions
and How to
Ace Them

◆

One may smile, and smile, and be a villain.

—William Shakespeare

Have you ever had an interviewer spring a question on you that was so tough your mind just went blank? You might have felt the question was so fraught with danger that a bomb had just dropped in your lap.

Here's a four-pronged approach that not only assures you'll give a great answer, but you'll look cool and self-assured as you do it. This is called the PACT Technique—Positive, Assure, Confess, Turn It Around—and it consistently works when the interviewee is faced with a no-win type of question.

PACT

POSITIVE

Even if the question asks you to reveal a weakness or is negative in any way, first say something positive. For example, if you are asked to tell about your supervisor's most disagreeable habit, you could start with one of these positions:

◆ "John was one of those rare people who was never disagreeable."

◆ "John delegated so well that if he had a disagreeable habit I guess I never picked up on it."

◆ "John had invested a lot in developing his managerial and interpersonal skills. There was really nothing habitual that he did that I found disagreeable."

It is imperative that your first response be extremely positive. The interviewer will be looking for your gut reaction. Be sure you look like a regular Pollyanna with nothing but good things to confess— at first.

Interviewers reason that if you didn't like the last boss, you might not like the new one after a few months. By really unloading on John for his disagreeable habit, you could come off looking difficult yourself.

No matter how negative a situation might have been in your past, you can always think of one positive thing to say about it. Dig deeply to come up with that one positive. Here are some troublesome questions and how you might begin your answer in a positive way.

QUESTION	UNVARNISHED TRUTH	POSITIVE FIRST RESPONSE
Would you characterize your former boss as hardworking?	John was a lazy dog. He dumped all his responsibilities on others. The only reason he kept his job was that he was always politicking instead of working.	John taught me how to work smarter. He fully utilized all his resources. That's just one of the things I learned from him. He took time to coach me in networking skills, and I learned how important it is to work hard yet work with others from various departments.
Do you mind travel?	I hate travel. I wish I were in another industry because travel will always be a part of my job. Why did I choose international sales?	I think people underestimate the upside of travel. Because I'm experienced at international travel, I know how to relax and get my rest on airplanes and in unfamiliar surroundings. I have young children at home and I really enjoy my weekends with them. I'll have to admit though, I often realize what a luxury it is to get caught up on my business reading in the peace and quiet of a hotel room. I come home a better dad, eager to devote my full attention to my family. For some families, the travel just works. We're one.

ASSURE, DON'T AVOID

Assure the interviewer that you will answer the question. Don't completely avoid it—that could trigger a negative response, especially if the interviewer has a controlling personality. Say something like the following:

◆ "I will answer this; however, nothing comes to mind quickly."

or

◆ "This is a tough one because John was such an easygoing person, but if you give me a second, I'll come up with an answer."

or

◆ "I'm not avoiding the question; I'm just trying to be as candid as possible."

If you completely blow off the question, a sharp interviewer will persist. The question will be asked over and over until you are forced to say something negative. Your best shot at coming off as the Prince Charming of interview candidates is to quickly assure the interviewer that you're going to give an answer—after your first *positive* response.

CONFESS

Divulge. Disclose. 'Fess up. This is what the interviewer is digging for. But be very selective in what you disclose. Here are the ABC's of confessing:

1. Confess only minor sins, weaknesses, or past indiscretions.

Example 1

Question: Have you ever been guilty of dishonesty on the job?

What to Confess: One time I wanted a promotion very much, but I was the least experienced member of our team. Our boss asked everyone interested to speak up. I said I wasn't interested because I thought I didn't have a chance. In hindsight I believe my boss wanted me to submit my application. I regret not being honest about wanting to apply. I learned from it. I'll be honest about things like that from now on, even if I risk failure.

Example 2
Question: *Tell me your greatest weakness.*

What to Confess: *I don't speak up when little things bother me. I've found most things blow over or work themselves out, so I'm not one to invest much energy. Still, by today's standards I should probably be more assertive.*

2. Confess something that the interviewer will think is not such a bad thing after all.

If asked about your weakness, confess something that makes you appear to be a saint.

Example:
One weakness I have is finding one software application and becoming so comfortable with it that I don't explore other programs. I've done that with MS Word. I've heard WordPerfect has some great features, but as long as I can produce good-looking reports with Word, I just don't experiment.

What a squeaky clean conscience you must have if this is your big confession. The interviewer is thinking:

◆ This guy is really tough on himself.

◆ This guy gets points for even thinking about experimenting with other programs.

- ◆ I'd be suspicious of a guy who had the leisure time to experiment.

- ◆ So, this guy does good-looking reports. We could use that on our team.

3. Confess something you know is not considered a sin in this corporate culture, but a badge of honor.

Example:

If you know that this corporation has the work ethic of Ebeneezer Scrooge and likes to squeeze long hours and hard labor out of its employees, you might answer the question about your greatest weakness like this:

I guess one area where I get carried away is in investing too much time in my projects—more than necessary. Especially when I get near the end of a project and I'm pulling together final reports and evaluations, I tend to put in unusually long hours, both early and late. It isn't a problem for me because I truly derive satisfaction from doing things in a really top-notch manner, but I know that's not a popular attitude today.

Your interviewer, if steeped in a workaholic culture, may rise from his chair and embrace you if you say this. Contrary to being a confession of guilt, you have cited your qualifications for brotherhood in this corporate family.

Caution:
Do your homework. Don't use an answer like this unless you're sure this company highly values hard work and long hours. If by mistake you are interviewing with a company that stresses balance, creativity, and a relaxed work ethic, you have doomed yourself by portraying yourself as such a hard worker.

You may raise red flags that you would be too demanding on your staff or that you might burn out quickly. Only in a culture that values grueling long hours can you get away with the above answer.

TURN IT AROUND
Take what you confess and turn it 180 degrees into a positive. The answer in the previous example starts with a confession but by the end it is turned into a positive.

Whatever you confess, the final part of your answer should actually make you look like a winner. You begin with a positive and end with a positive.

METHODS OF TURNING NEGATIVE QUESTIONS INTO POSITIVES

◆ *Happy Ending.* Show that the mistake resulted in your learning new skills or changing industries. Show that this change is what perfectly suits you for the job you have today. If the weakness you confess is that you become so engrossed in your research you tune out everything around you, that could be a good thing if

- the position you seek is a market research analyst.

- the interviewer is looking for someone who can work unsupervised in a cubicle environment.

After confessing that you tune out, state that this habit has helped you produce more reports than any other market analyst at your current company. That's a happy ending for anyone interested in hiring you!

◆ *Weakness Becomes a Strength.* Go a step further. Show that you have actually become a star in the area that was once a weakness. In an earlier question, the interviewee confessed that he once was not assertive enough. To show that not only is he not weak in this area now, but he has actually become a star, he might say something like:

No one would ever believe that assertiveness was once a problem for me. I am considered our department's strongest negotiator with vendors. Last year alone, I reduced our cost of consumable items by 10 percent through vendor negotiations.

What a way to finish with an impressive flourish! Don't fear negative questions—they are door openers in disguise for bragging about yourself. You just have to learn to work your way from a negative to a positive.

◆ *Sins of Youth.* State that the mistake you made was in your youth or during your first year of business or in a part-time high school job. Laugh at what a callow youth you were.

SUMMARY OF PACT TECHNIQUE
Remember this PACT for coming up with fabulous answers that win jobs:

P = POSITIVE	Your first response should bring up the one positive thing you can think of on this topic.
A = ASSURE (Don't avoid)	Assure the interviewer that you are about to answer the question. Don't completely avoid the question, or the interviewer could become hostile.
C = CONFESS	Confess minor things or things that could actually be viewed as positives. Be very, very careful what you confess.
T = TURN IT AROUND	Take the weakness or problems you confessed and show how this actually was an asset. Show how a weakness when you were young has become your greatest strength. End the answer with a positive note—a happy ending. Prove to the interviewer that you are an even better candidate than ever, based on this answer.

Chapter 4

---◆---

No-Win Questions, Thorny Dilemmas, and Catch-22s

◆

Problems are only opportunities in work clothes.

—Henry J. Kaiser

DO YOU STILL CHEAT ON YOUR TAXES?

This question illustrates how to put the respondent in an impossible situation. If the answering person feels he must give a Yes or a No answer, he winds up looking like a loser either way. Questions such as this one are set up to force you to take one of two possibly unpopular positions. They are carefully laid traps designed by interviewers to pressure you into saying something negative. You may feel that no matter which of the two avenues you take, you are going to look like a jerk. Here are some suggestions for answering these slippery questions in a way that makes you look like a star.

TURN IT AROUND
Example:

Any kind of tax evasion is inappropriate. I am scrupulous about reporting income, even the value of air miles and other perks. My ethics and values are very important to me.

◆ The answer above starts with something that no one can argue with: Tax evasion is inappropriate.

◆ The answer quickly focuses on a specific example of something positive the respondent does—reporting all income, even air miles. It is easier to talk about one specific example than to articulate your philosophy. Besides, your philosophy may not be the same as the interviewer's.

◆ The answer does not sound defensive or apologetic. Sounding very positive is key to pulling off a great response. One could easily be offended by this insensitive question. Instead, the answer is conversational and interesting.

The following are the strategies to follow for answering seemingly no-win questions.

Strategies

1. Don't get boxed into Yes-No answers.

2. Even if you do, don't give a simple Yes or No.

3. Agree with what's obvious. Agree strongly. Begin with a statement that no one can disagree with, such as a value or a popular sentiment.

4. Give yourself an out.

5. Get focused on a specific example. Don't spend a lot of time philosophizing.

6. State something positive about yourself, preferably an accomplishment. This should be very concrete, not subjective.

EXERCISE

How will you respond when the interviewer asks you a question like "Do you still cheat on your taxes?"

Write a response to one of the following interview questions.

Question: What's your strength—quality work or working within a budget?

Answer: Being committed both to quality and to the bottom line are required of managers today. Perhaps my achievements in Total Quality Management and in production have led you to believe that budget was not my focus, but I was committed to cost control. I came within or under budget on every project I undertook for McDermott. A strong manager can manage both cost and quality simultaneously.

The interviewer will get so caught up in the specifics of your answer that there is a really good chance that she won't realize that you haven't allowed yourself to be forced to take a position on this question. If she pushes, you can always resort to the ultimate fall-back answer:

The Ultimate Fallback Answer
I would have to take each situation on its merits. Judging each situation on a case-by-case basis would help me make the appropriate decision. The primary factors that I would take into consideration include these:

◆ Who are all the stakeholders?

◆ What are the consequences of either choice?

◆ What are the benefits of each choice?

Question: If you had a difficult project to do in a short amount of time, what would be more important to you—meeting that deadline no matter what, or doing a quality job even if you had to work past the deadline?

Answer: I assume that if a manager gives me a deadline, that deadline is important to a total plan or process, so I take it very seriously. Quality, however, must be maintained. In emergencies like this I follow a three-point plan to assure that I deliver a quality product on time. First, I start with the deadline and work backwards to design a schedule that assures completion. Second, I call on my resources—my teammates and my staff—to help. Finally, I commit to putting in the extra time it takes to do a rush job like this. Everyone in a company should expect the unexpected to happen once in a while and be willing to pitch in. Being flexible about these things is critical to the way we work today and actually increases my job satisfaction.

When you use a number like "three-point plan," you sound impressive, smart, and prepared to meet the job's challenges. Be careful, however. You must be sure to have three points and not two if you begin this way. If you ever have trouble thinking of that third one while you are on the spot, use the phrase "communicating to your boss or subordinates or peers" as a fallback.

Question: In what area could you benefit from developing and improving?

Answer: I actually have an ongoing plan for my professional development. The current developmental step I am taking is learning Spanish. One of my former bosses told me about our company's projections of hiring more Hispanic workers. I want to be better prepared for our more global workplace, no matter what company employs me. Learning Spanish is my first step in preparing myself.

This answer is great on so many levels. Not only do you look strategic in your thinking by taking Spanish, you also accomplish the following:

◆ You demonstrate openness to diversity.

◆ You compliment your former boss—always a good move.

◆ You show that you have initiative to develop yourself and don't expect spoon-feeding.

◆ You confess to a weakness that really isn't a weakness but just one more strength.

Way to go!

WATCH OUT FOR SECONDARY QUESTIONS!

Do not be surprised if, after you deliver a great answer, the interviewer continues to grill you or appears not to understand your answer. Often, if you give a really great answer, the interviewer will probe further to try to ruffle your composure. These secondary questions are tough, because you have already answered the question beautifully the first time. Here are a few of the secondary questions you may be asked about your answer.

1. What do you mean by that?

2. What trends?

3. [Silence]

4. Tell me more about ____.

5. In what sense?

6. Explain what you mean by ____.

If this happens to you, remember that showing that you can respond in a friendly manner without losing your composure is more important than anything you say. Your impulse will be to be frustrated with these questions, but you must act as if this is a question you welcome. To answer, you may do one of the following:

◆ Paraphrase your last answer.

◆ Give another example. Say, "I can illustrate by sharing this example."

◆ Define a term or word you used. "By vertical marketing, I mean contacting new utilities since we are already marketing to utilities."

Good news! If you are being grilled with secondary questions, that simply means that you have done very well on your initial response. Since your first answer was flawless, the interviewer is being forced to go back in with a secondary question to uncover any weakness!

Chapter 5

Questions About Past and Current Jobs

◆

It is not I that belong to the past, but that the past belongs to me.

—Mary Antin

Don't be surprised if one of your initial questions is a very general question about your most recent job. Your attitude and work habits in that job are the best indicators of how successfully you will perform for the potential new employer. *Do not waste this valuable opportunity.*

These rather generic first questions about your job are great opportunities to showcase your experience and expertise. The questions are so open that you can pull in almost anything you choose to brag about.

BILLBOARD ANSWERS

Billboard answers are short, memorable one-liners that describe your experience, accomplishments, or anything about you that might impress an interviewer. Use the brief, clear style you might use if you were to put your fine traits on a billboard. After all, you are selling a product—you. People today are so used to seeing products portrayed in the high-impact style of short bits and bytes that you must describe yourself this way if you are to make a lasting impression.

Before you go to any interview, you should prepare at least three billboard phrases. Determine ahead of time that you will attempt to drop these juicy tidbits about your past accomplishments or work history.

Examples:

◆ "I led the department in new accounts opened."

◆ "My team maintained more overhead lights than any team in the state although we were no larger than the other teams."

◆ "When I headed Operations, we won the Deming Award for Quality."

◆ "My background in sales as well as research uniquely qualifies me for this position."

◆ "Complaints shrank by 10 percent when I assumed the manager's position."

◆ "We met 110 percent of our goals—meeting all goals plus more than 10 percent of our projections."

TYPICAL QUESTIONS

The following are some typical questions you may be asked about your current or past job. If you are currently employed, apply these questions to your current position. If not, apply them to your last job. Some are just different ways of asking for the same information, so they are grouped together.

> **Note:** In this list and all following lists, there is only one answer to a whole group of similar questions. The answer will be tailored to the last question in the list. You can adapt it to work for the other questions that are phrased somewhat differently.

GENERAL

In these questions, you may or may not be asked about your success and accomplishments. Your answers, however, should showcase your success and accomplishments. Don't just tell your responsibilities; even a loser had those. Tell what you contributed.

Questions:

1. Tell me about your present (last) position.

2. If I were to ask your former supervisor, what would she say your contributions were to the department?

3. What did it take to be successful in your last position? Be specific.

4. Why do you think you were successful in your last job?

Answer: There were three things that I was proudest of in my last job. First, our department improved our customer satisfaction rating measurably, based on the Holman Customer Satisfaction Survey. Second, we went from being six individual contributors to working as a team. The mutual support we gave each other on projects helped everyone achieve some pretty remarkable results. Finally, the department had previously had a reputation for poor internal customer service. After my first few months on the job, managers began e-mailing my vice president thanking him for the improved service to internal customers. This was considered a complete turnaround for this department in less than a year.

CAREER

Questions:

1. Tell me about your career up till now.

2. Tell me a little about yourself.

Spend very little time discussing your early career if you have a long work history. Focus on the jobs that relate to this position. Devote more time to recent positions and accomplishments.

Answer: Although I have more than 25 years' experience, all of it has related to this position in one way or another. My first job was teaching high school math. That constant preparation for lectures and presentations still helps me today to prepare for presentations to executive managers. When I left teaching and entered the work-force, I was at first a market analyst, supporting the marketing professionals. I quickly was promoted to marketing representative and then senior marketing representative. In that position, I led my team in total revenue managed and I was often acknowledged by winning such things as the New Products Sales Contest and the Summer Sizzle Sales Drive. I once opened 30 new accounts in one month. That led to my being offered the position of sales manager. Since taking that position last May, I have instituted new revenue streams via the Internet, strengthened our interdepartmental sup-port, and increased total revenue by more than $40,000.

If you don't have a lot of jobs to talk about, use specific tasks and examples from any jobs you do have.

Answer: One part of my experience that probably best prepared me for management was managing my own business. I started my own lawn maintenance service that paid my personal expenses through-out high school and college. It taught me about cash flow, capital investments, and planning ahead. After graduation, I began my career with Equifax as a Customer Information Representative. I received three commendations my first year for exceptional cus-tomer service. Soon I became team leader for our staff of five. I supervise the flow of work, motivate individual employees, moni-tor results, and give constructive feedback as needed. The produc-tion of our team has increased measurably since my designation as team leader, according to our monthly production reports.

QUALITIES AND STRENGTHS

Question: What was your greatest accomplishment in your last (current) job?

Answer: I worked with a team that supported me so well that I had lots of opportunities for accomplishment, so it's difficult to say which was greatest. I would have to choose between either achieving a record high in total sales revenue or in overhauling the commission structure so that there were incentives for people to work as a team as well as to contribute individually. Both were good for the company and good for my teammates.

Question: What interpersonal skills are your strengths? Which would you like to improve?

Answer: Interpersonal skills are a strength of mine, so let me think. We can all improve, so I'd like to improve in any way I can, even if I am already skilled in an area. I suppose I'd like to improve my nonverbal communication. I'd like to be more expressive and learn a wider range of nonverbal communication that would show my teammates my support even when I am not saying a word, as in meetings while they are presenting.

Question: If I were to ask your former supervisor, what would she say are your strengths?

Answer: My supervisor really deserves a lot of credit for bringing out these strengths in me so this is actually a credit to her. I know she had talked to our vice president about my ability to think strategically, because he chose me to be on a team that put together our strategic plan. Second, she always noted on my performance evaluations that I was consistent in meeting deadlines, which are very aggressive in our business. The strength that she probably valued most is that I am a bridge builder between people. Whenever there were two people with differing points of view, whether they were my peers or customers, I was able to see both sides and find workable solutions. This helped her get her job done faster and with fewer headaches that got passed up the chain of command to her.

REASONS FOR LEAVING LAST JOB

This is tricky. You have to give acceptable reasons for leaving and here are some of them:

◆ You finished a degree, a course of training, or other developmental milestone.

◆ You made a conscious decision to try a new field: sales, training, human resources.

◆ It was a strategic move to prepare you for the workforce of the future.

◆ You wanted upward mobility (but don't appear *too* mobile or *too* ambitious).

◆ Relocation (but make sure the interviewer knows you're planning a permanent move).

Questions:

1. What could have happened differently in your last job that would have avoided your sitting here today?

2. Give me your reasons for leaving your previous job.

Answer: I have been a corporate trainer and speaker for more than ten years. I believe there exist new and exciting opportunities to share training and information using the Internet. This job with your company would place me right where I want to be—in a job that develops my Internet expertise. I look forward to making this change and keeping my skills current.

or

Answer: My leaving was really not about the job I had but about the next step I wanted to make in my career. I wanted to move into sales. When I surveyed the market, I realized that the greatest opportunities would probably be in telecommunications. That is why I want to join your company—ATT is a leader in this industry.

DISSATISFACTION WITH LAST JOB

All of the questions below are after a common goal: to make you disclose a weakness of your own. Although they ask questions about what was wrong with your last job, they really are trying to read between the lines to find out what is wrong with you. Employers don't want a disgruntled employee who will leave them after the initial investment in training. Be cautious. Be entirely positive. Review S.S.S. and read Chapter 3 carefully.

Questions:

1. Why did you leave your last job?

2. Why are you thinking of leaving your current job?

3. What was lacking in your last job that you hope to find?

4. What part of your job challenges you because it is difficult? How do you deal with this?

5. Pretend that you can redesign your current (last) job. Describe the changes you would make.

6. Have you altered your job description? In what way?

7. What did you dislike about your last job?

Answer: It's not that I disliked anything about my job; in fact, I really enjoyed it. If I had to say something along those lines, I guess I'd just say that there were so many opportunities to provide new types of customer service through products and solutions, and I just couldn't pursue them all. Of course, I took great satisfaction in achieving and exceeding existing goals, but I sometimes wished there were more hours in a day to pursue new opportunities.

I was able to launch our web site and I implemented many of the opportunities I saw. Although my management was extremely satisfied with what I accomplished, I'd like to have had time to do more innovation.

FAVORITE TASKS

Note that the next three questions appear to be very positive. They are not. In a backhanded way, they are eliciting from you what you don't like. Here are a few of the things interviewers are trying to see if you will have problems with, if they hire you.

◆ hard work

◆ teamwork

◆ authority

◆ travel, long hours, work habits

◆ burnout

◆ self-motivation

By saying what you *do* like, you may reveal what you *don't* like. For example, you might say, "I liked working as a sales rep because I made my own schedule and didn't have to get into the rush hour traffic in the mornings. I could make calls from home." To some interviewers, you might be revealing traits that might not make you a good candidate for a more structured job that requires increased time in the office.

If you said your favorite part of your job was being solely responsible for writing the business plan and that you would sometimes write for four or five days at a time, then you might be revealing that you are a loner rather than a team player. If you are interviewing for a position that requires you to work alone, this is a good answer, but if you are expected to function in a work group, this answer is a loser. Above all, your answer needs to show you are well rounded and skilled in every part of the job. Note how the answer that follows these questions gives the business plan experience a different, more positive spin.

Questions:

1. What did you like about your [last / current] job?

2. What was your favorite job? Why?

3. What part of your job do you do best? Why?

Answer: I really have a great job, so I suppose the one part I would choose as my favorite would be writing the business plan. Creating the plan allows me to do the three things I enjoy most: work with other team members to get their contributions and perspective, use my organizational skills to put the information into a format that will be meaningful to the Executive Committee, and use my creativity to take raw information and create a strategic plan from just facts and statistics.

PAST PERFORMANCE PROBLEMS

The key here is to have a positive first response regarding your former employer.

Questions:

1. What would your former boss say are your developmental areas?

2. How have your previous jobs made you a better employee (manager, instructor)?

Answer: I had a great boss who really believed in development. One thing he did was invest in sending us to courses to update our computer skills. It is a developmental area for me and spending that time has made me better at my job.

MERGERS AND CHANGES

Question: Why do you think you were chosen as one of the employees to be discharged during the downsizing?

Answer: Our industry is changing for the better. One thing that will allow us to provide better service at a lower cost to customers is our merger with Suntrust. There are economies of scale that are very advantageous to our customers. Naturally, there was some duplication of talent when the merger took place and my position was just one of the positions that needed to be eliminated due to this duplication. This is a great opportunity for me to get into another [company / industry]. As a student of the business, I believe that this move will actually benefit me by broadening the scope of my experience.

TECHNICAL
Questions:

1. Did you feel that your former company dealt effectively with technology?

2. Did your former company invest enough in technology and/or equipment?

Answer: There is new equipment and technology coming on the market every day. No company can afford to go out and invest in every new technology that comes along. Information Systems managers like me would certainly never say no to management wanting to invest more in technology. We can always find useful ways to invest those budget dollars. One investment that my former company made at my recommendation was to fully switch over to DSL. That enabled me to increase the productivity of my work group by at least 12 percent.

SALES
Question: What are some problems that you feel are typical for sales professionals?

Answer: A successful midmarket sales professional learns early on to schedule time for three important tasks: preparation of materials and presentations, face-to-face customer contact, and follow-up and phone time. Leaving out any one of these can weaken one's total number of sales. Consistent sales success is simply a matter of having a plan for each day that allows the appropriate amount of time to take care of all of these tasks. It's not difficult if you get into good habits of planning your work and working your plan.

Chapter 6

Questions About Education, Development, and Other Assets

◆

*Life is my college. May I graduate well, and
earn some honours!*

—Louisa May Alcott

One of the things that the interviewer will look at on your résumé
will be your education. Do you have the credentials required for
this position? For some jobs in such fields as medicine or architec-
ture, the degrees or training are nonnegotiable. For some other
positions, however, you can make your background even more
impressive by the way you answer questions.

Education today is not limited to degrees and formal training.
Employers are looking to see if you have shown initiative in your
own professional development. This development may be anything
from sprucing up your image to learning Chinese.

VALUABLE ASSETS
What are some of the things that are impressing interviewers
today?

The following are considered valuable assets in many companies. If
you have these abilities, drop them into the interview. You may
have to take the lead and mention them if the interviewer doesn't
ask. Think ahead of time of ways you can bring these up when you
are asked about your education, professionalism, or activities.

◆ *Proposal/Report Writing.* Can you write a good report? Pro-
posal? Business plan?

◆ *Second Language.* Do you speak a second language? Are you taking lessons? This is a hot commodity in today's job market. Spanish and Chinese are two of many recommended languages.

◆ *Self-Starter.* Say things to show that you have a history of taking the initiative. Give an example of a proactive approach you took to your job or a situation.

◆ *Technology.* Get all the technology expertise you can. Currently, the use of DVD, DSL, intranet services, and web services are hot. By the time of this book's printing, there will be a dozen new technologies. Stay current.

◆ *Rotations.* Have you spent time working outside your field in order to broaden your perspective about your industry or company? Spending time in another department or job can be a real eye-opener. This rotation is particularly valuable if you have worked in an area that you will be serving.

Example:

Tony Barge is an excellent example of how this experience can be developmental. He worked in sales in a large electric utility. The Operations engineers were constantly complaining because Tony would sign contracts with customers to install systems and run lines for incredibly low prices. Then he would often throw in a free service or monitoring device just to close the deal. The Operations people were under constraints to work within a budget, and Tony's impulsive freebies made it difficult for them to meet their annual budget goals. Tony was sent to work in Operations for six months as part of his professional development. He personally found it impossible to work within the budget when the sales force began using his old tactics of giveaways to win customers. Tony did not meet budget, and his performance incentive pay was reduced because of it. When he returned to sales, he was much more conservative about giving away the company store.

QUESTIONS: EDUCATION AND DEVELOPMENT

Companies know that one of the keys to remaining competitive in today's market is to have well-trained employees. Paradoxically, companies are trimming training and development budgets drastically as a means of delivering short-term shareholder value.

Today's employers are looking for lifelong learners who can change as they change, grow as they grow.

What does this mean to the professional employee seeking a position? Here is what employers are looking for:

◆ Employers want to see that you have kept current with your training and development.

◆ Employers don't want to bear all the costs of your professional development; they look for signs that you are also willing to invest.

◆ Employers want to see evidence that you are willing to grow. Are you flexible enough to adapt to new skills needed for today and for tomorrow? Do you embrace change?

◆ Employers want to see that you are creative in your pursuit of professional development. Have you done anything besides traditional corporate seminars? Have you tried peer training, cross-training, Internet training, or mentoring?

The following questions reflect the balance that employers seek in the area of training and development. They want employees to pursue training and development, but they don't want to invest too many lost man-hours or too much money on costly training programs. These questions help the interviewer determine if you have a proactive but balanced approach to development.

GENERAL

If possible, make whatever answer you give reflect the fact that you are very current and forward thinking in your training. For example, if your answer to the following question is some management training you took 20 years ago, your interviewer may think your skills are somewhat stale. Perhaps that training really is the most valuable training you have ever had. Still, could you function today without the updates to your computer skills, or could you hire appropriately without the interviewing skills you have learned?

Consider giving as your answer a type of nontraditional training such as having been mentored by a vice president or taking a course through software that you purchased at Staples. Whatever you do, make the course or intervention sound valuable because it helped contribute to the bottom line and not just to you personally.

Question: What is the single most valuable training or development experience you have ever had?

Answer: One of the most valuable developmental moves I have made recently was subscribing to *getAbstract.com*. I'm a believer in keeping up with the latest management literature and have gained productive ideas from many of the best-sellers I have read through the years. The problem is that there is so much good literature available and so little time.

Question: How do you feel about job rotations—spending weeks, months, perhaps a year in another area of your company in order to develop you into a better-rounded employee?

Answer: I am open to any type of developmental move that will help me perform better in my current position or prepare me to serve in another area in the company as I grow in experience. Job rotations do both of those things. First, they help employees understand how their function fits with the overall business plan of the company and the needs of other internal stakeholders. Second, these rotations often introduce the employee to other positions in the company that they may eventually aspire to. Rotations can be a win-win for the employee and the company.

FUTURE DEVELOPMENT

Question: If you could do one developmental thing for yourself, what would it be? This could include training or other developmental experiences.

> **Note:** *This is a hot answer right now.*

Answer: In fact, I am pursuing a developmental experience right now outside the company. I am learning Spanish as a second language to prepare me for communicating with Hispanic customers and vendors. The way the Internet and other forces have made the workplace global so quickly, I believe that a second language will soon be a requirement for management. I want to be prepared.

Question: What educational plans, if any, do you have for the future? Why?

Answer: Returning to school at night to finish my MBA is my plan at this time. Of course, my plans will be influenced by the career move I make next. Many universities now offer MBAs through Saturday-only classes. If travel or evening hours make night courses unfeasible, I will pursue weekend classes or a distance learning program. I consider having a graduate degree part of my total professional development. It's also a great way to bring back to my job cutting-edge ideas through the professors, who are often consultants to top companies. Another valuable part of an MBA program is pooling ideas with other students who are currently managers.

or

Answer: Although I already have a graduate degree, I intend to continue my education in a variety of ways. My current developmental project involves enrolling with a business writing coach who teaches managers to improve their writing skills online. I want to learn to polish and perfect reports and business plans.

WHOSE RESPONSIBILITY IS TRAINING AND DEVELOPMENT?

These questions are fraught with danger. You should sound open to any developmental suggestions made by your employer. On the other hand, you shouldn't sound as if you expect a free ride to a lot of training classes or that you will miss too many days of work pursuing development. Show that you will bear much of the responsibility and costs of your development, but that you are willing to be molded.

Questions:

1. How much do you think a company should invest in developing employees?

2. Who is responsible for professional development?

3. Who should guide your professional development?

Answer: Although many companies are good about developing people, ultimately employees are responsible for much of their own development. Through performance appraisals and good communication on the job, employees can always identify ways to improve and grow. If the company offers courses or coaching to help employees, that's always appreciated. If, however, employees have developmental needs that the company isn't equipped to address, they should invest in their own development.

Answer—for managers who may be expected to develop others. Use the answer above and add the following: As a manager, I use mentoring and coaching daily as part of my way of developing people. I am also a big believer in peer coaching. I often pair up employees who have diverse strengths and have them coach each other. One employee may be very good technically and the other may be better at communicating with our internal customers. I give them time during slow periods to train one another and observe. It's great development and costs the company less time and money than traditional training.

DANGEROUS QUESTIONS

These questions actually are sneaky ways to find out your weaknesses. Often, employees go to training to strengthen an area of weakness. Your answer should state that you sought training and development as icing on the cake for your already considerable talents. Never admit a weakness if you don't have to.

Another tactic is to focus consistently on the future. If you are seeking training and development for a skill needed in the future, then you appear proactive and smart.

Question: What is your plan for professional development?

Answer: I am trying to learn skills to prepare me for working in the more competitive market we will be facing soon. My plan includes subscribing to one new industry periodical that I will read to keep up on changes in our industry beyond just the company I work for. And I plan to learn videoconferencing skills. Videoconferencing is a great way to save money and time.

Question: What have you done for your professional development in the last year?

Answer: Making presentations has always been a part of my job that I excel at and enjoy. I wanted to see if I could get pointers and feedback from experienced speakers. On my own time, I joined Toastmasters and have attended several lectures and seminars that have given me great ideas.

WHY DID YOU . . . ?

> **Remember:** Never admit to a mistake in an interview. Package everything you ever did as a contribution to preparing you for this job.

Questions:

1. Why did you decide to go to graduate school?

2. Why did you major in sociology (science / education)? (This question may be asked if your major appears not to relate to the job.)

Answer: The discipline of studying sociology has helped me approach every new job and even new projects with an objectivity I learned from that major. I have learned to look at all the facts, all the trends, and all the information instead of just winging it. Much of this job is decision making and problem solving. Studying sociology taught me to gather information to make good decisions based on the facts.

Psychology can teach you about working with people; drama can teach you to make great presentations and communicate with others; computer science can help you deal with technology from vendors and peers in other departments, and soon. You can always find a way your old major or your graduate studies will make you more qualified for *this* position.

Question: Why did you select this career?

Answer: This career helps me capitalize on my two greatest strengths: communicating with others and organizational skills. Managing others (training, selling) requires directing them in a very positive and clear way. I can do that; in fact, I enjoy that. So those positive influencing skills I have are put to good use every day. Also, I am a strong organizer. That means that I use such resources as time, people, and services efficiently and economically.

Take, for instance, last year's sales meeting. I coordinated the entire event. First I went on-line to comparison price everything from catering to hotels to speakers. Then I divided up my staff to look into the quality offered by the various vendors. We all got back together later and made the decisions about what to do, where to stay, and so on by consensus. The sales meeting was the top-rated one in company history due to good organization and communications.

Questions:

1. Why did you choose this company?

2. Why did you choose your last job?

Note: The answers to these two questions must stress your strengths and compliment the companies involved.

Answer: I chose my last job for three reasons: First, the company was in healthcare, which I believe will be a growing industry due to our aging population (mention any positive industry trend). Second, the job offered me a chance to manage technology, which is something I do well. The position allowed me to develop my experience further because the department was a large one. Finally, I believe one should take a job because it's appealing and will offer job satisfaction. The job can be the greatest in the world, but if you're not doing what brings you fulfillment, then the fit will not be good for you or the company. I just really wanted that job—just like I really want this job.

> **Note:** Add the last item about job satisfaction only if you remained satisfied in your last job for at least two years.

Question: If you could do it all over again, what would you major in?

Answer: I probably would major in the same thing—education. Part of any job I have held in industry has been educating others: customers, vendors, and staff. That training has helped me get people up to speed in a productive and timely manner that seems to be appreciated. I know how to deal with all kinds of people because I have learned that various learning styles take in information differently, and I can adapt.

The technical part of this job must be updated constantly. Even if I had earned a degree in engineering ten years ago, the information would now be out of date. What I learned about leading and supporting people through my education degree, however, is just as valid today.

or

Answer: Even though I no longer do the engineering, I would still major in engineering. The staff and customers know that I speak their language and have empathy for their issues. I'm amazed at how helpful it is to me, even today, that I have that degree. With some of the people we serve, it's a door opener and a type of common ground.

Chapter 7

---◆---

Questions About the Past

◆

We have to do with the past only as we can make it useful to the present and the future.

—Frederick Douglass

RESUME RED FLAGS AND DISCREPANCIES

Do you have a spot in your résumé that might raise questions or concerns for the interviewer? Are there any gaps in time between one job and the next? Be prepared to account for any unusual items or omissions when you come to the interview.

Question: You have no experience listed here from 1992 to 1993. Why?

The very best answer, if possible, is something concrete that contributes to your skills or expertise. (These responses, though, could appear on your résumé, and there would *be* no gaps.)

Answers:

◆ I was attending the Schuller Management Institute.

◆ I was getting an MBA.

◆ I wanted to learn Portuguese so I could negotiate with the Brazilians; therefore, I went there to live for a year.

Barring something that makes sense like the above, you can try an answer like the ones below that makes your unemployed year sound like a totally constructive experience.

or

Answer: When our bank merged and my position as controller was terminated, I decided that this was the perfect time to reassess my career, review my goals, and really invest in myself as a professional. I didn't want to just jump at the first opportunity that came along. I wanted to look at what I wanted for my career long term. That is why I am very sure that this is the position for which I am perfectly suited. The career counseling I invested in plus my own review of this industry confirm that I could make a real contribution here, and derive a great deal of career satisfaction from the job.

or

Answer: I had read that many executives had taken sabbaticals just before their most productive and memorable periods in their careers. I decided not to wait until I was an executive. I spent a year looking at the industry from the outside, studying the various companies I might want to work for, and establishing my priorities in my career. I returned to the workplace much more focused and fully committed to making a real contribution to this industry.

Answers to Avoid:

◆ "I took time off to be with my children." Yes, that should be acceptable, but if your children are still young, you might lose out on an opportunity if you say this. If your youngest child has started school, you can use this answer. The key is to make the interviewer feel totally assured that the child-rearing issue is completely in the past, tidily squared away.

◆ "[I / my parents / my husband] had some health problems."

◆ "I went through some [difficult times / depression / personal problems] and took some time off."

◆ "I just got burned out in sales, but I am fine now."

◆ "No one was hiring in the airline industry that year."

◆ "I actively sought a job, but things just didn't click. Timing is half of it."

Note: Your interviewer is not allowed to discriminate against you based on your gender, race, marital status, or other similar criteria. If he does, consider saying politely, not sharply: "I am the best person for the job and will meet or exceed your expectations." Say what you have to offer, but don't be defensive.

Question: I see you made a career switch here from management into sales. What happened?

Concentrate on what you went to and not what you left. Concentrate on the positives of the new and not the negative aspects of the old. The best answer is that the new position was a promotion or step up the ladder. If that were not the case, try an answer like the following:

Answer: I love sales. Selling is my talent and I enjoy doing it every day. Although I had been successful as a manager and had great performance reviews, I just didn't enjoy it as much as selling. Also, in some ways, the opportunities are greater in sales.

What Not to Say:

◆ "I like making my own schedule and the independence."

◆ "I don't like the paperwork of management."

◆ "I don't like bureaucracy."

◆ "I don't like working in an office all day."

Question: You attended Cornell for three years, but then graduated from the University of Maryland. Why the change?

Answer: The University of Maryland offered some courses in real estate finance that I could not get at Cornell. I was very attracted to UM's program and thought it was worth the switch.

Question: You left BellSouth for five years but came back in 1989. Tell me about that.

Answer: The only work experience I had ever had was at BellSouth. I felt that while I was young, and before I needed to make a real commitment, I should try to get a different perspective as part of my professional development. The experience turned out to be very valuable. I came back more committed to BellSouth than ever because I saw for myself what a great company it is.

Question: I see that you worked for three years as a technical writer (substitute a different position), yet your résumé shows no formal writing (substitute a different skill) training. How did that happen?

Answer: Thanks to a tremendously talented manager in my first job, who taught me to write technical proposals and reports, I became known for turning out great technical documents that were highly effective internally and externally. I seemed to have a natural talent for it and my manager developed that talent. Because I had achieved successful results, Corporate Communications offered me a position as a technical writer. I learned even more from them, so I *was* educated—just not in traditional coursework.

Question: You have several jobs that you've kept for only a year or two. What will happen when you master this job and it becomes less challenging?

Answer: Early in a person's career, I think it helps to explore various opportunities. That way, when you reach a point when building a career at one company becomes your goal, you can choose the best company for you. Many people experience burnout or become stale because they have worked for the same company throughout their careers. I have looked at the market from the inside of several companies. Now, I am at that point of wanting to build a career, and Compaq is the company I have identified as my top choice.

Question: Why did you leave General Motors after only 18 months?

Answer: My experience with General Motors was great. I learned their system of managing for productivity, which I think will always be valuable to me. Still, I was younger and had not fully committed to making General Motors the company in which I would build my career. When Sara Lee offered me the opportunity to learn to manage technology as a senior manager, it was a once-in-a-lifetime opportunity. I knew that learning to manage technology would make me more valuable as a manager and employee. It was rather like going to graduate school because I learned so much. After much thought, I decided that this was a move I should make.

Note that the candidate first makes it clear that she had good reasons for leaving other than money. Second, she compliments General Motors to answer the hidden question here: "Did you leave General Motors because of any problems?" Finally, she assures the interviewer that she was very young and that she gave the move a lot of thought because she is not a job hopper, the interviewer's real fear here.

Chapter 8

Questions to
Detect Your
Weaknesses

◆

The real fault is to have faults and not amend them.

—Confucius

If you were hiring someone, wouldn't you want to know his or her weaknesses? Your potential employers want this information as well. They are not out to get you; they just don't want to make a mistake.

Everyone has a weakness somewhere—you just don't have to tell all about it in a job interview. Here are the cardinal rules when asked about your weaknesses:

◆ Don't confess too much.

◆ Don't confess at all, if possible.

◆ If you are forced to name a weakness, name a small one or one that might actually be considered a virtue by the employer.

◆ Never volunteer information about a weakness or mistake.

◆ Distance yourself in some way from any past mistake.

The following answers will show you how to handle this extremely difficult but inevitable part of the interview.

GENERAL
Question: If you could wave a magic wand and have one personal trait or quality strengthened, what would that be?

Answer: I have a personality that works effectively with a wide range of people, so I don't think I would want to make a drastic change. I guess I would just like the opportunity to work with a wider range of people so that I could gain even more experience working with others. I believe that every person I meet has something to teach me, so working with the new group in this position would offer me an opportunity to get to know many new people and learn something from each one.

Questions:

1. What are your weaknesses? How have you strengthened them?

2. In what areas would you like to improve?

Answer: As our industry changes and new technologies evolve, I hope I never stop learning. Although there is not a specific weakness, I will say that there is always something new to learn. By reading current business periodicals, I become aware of new technologies or new trends in management and I want to learn more about them. I suppose right now that we have yet to explore all the capabilities of the Internet as a management tool. Although I use the Internet for many tasks already, I'd like to learn more about applications other managers and executives have found.

Question: In what areas have you seen improvement in your performance or development?

> **Note:** Don't admit a weakness. Instead, say that you have gained experience. Of course, you have gained experience through the years. No one can find fault with that.

Answer: [Management / Nursing / Teaching] came naturally to me. Still, I suppose what has improved me is the seasoning that comes with experience. Although I could always rely on my good instincts and training, as the years go by I have much more confidence because of my experience. Decisions are easier because I have successfully worked through similar situations in the past.

WEAKNESSES SPECIFIC TO A NEW POSITION
Questions:

1. What parts of this job will be unfamiliar to you? How will you deal with that?

2. What training do you anticipate needing to perform this job well?

Answer: Because of my previous experience with Canada Life, I expect to be a contributor from the beginning. I look forward to the information and experience my teammates have to share. There may also be some operational or technical information you may have to introduce me to as I will be new to the company. As far as my professional abilities, however, I am prepared for this job and hope to be a productive part of this team from the outset.

It's okay to mention some minor task that you will have to learn:

◆ how to operate a piece of equipment.

◆ security measures unique to this company.

◆ understanding the hierarchy or organizational structure.

◆ the definition of a new territory.

PROBLEMS IN LAST JOB
Questions:

1. In what area would your [teammates / supervisor] say you could improve?

2. What could have happened differently that would have kept you in your current or most recent job?

3. Why do you want to change jobs?

4. What are your reasons for leaving?

If you are applying for a position that is at a higher level you may say this:

Answer: A recent study of our company revealed that there would be virtually no growth opportunities for managers at my level for several years. There are just no slots at Williamson Brothers for me to take that next step. Your company offers this position for which I am fully qualified and could succeed in now. I am ready and this is the right position.

or

Answer: Your company is larger and is a place where I could build a career. Although I really enjoy what I do, for the long term I want to be somewhere that will eventually offer opportunities for those who succeed and offer consistent performance.

Do not use the above answers if this is a lateral move; instead, adapt one of the following to your needs:

Answer: I am very interested in your work with vegetable dyes. It's exciting and I'd like to be a part of that team.

Other acceptable reasons:

◆ You like their location better for some reason (proximity to family, the beach).

◆ They are an industry leader and you want to join.

◆ Their equipment or facility is better.

Question: To what lengths should a company go to check with former employers?

> **Note:** Be in favor of this. Show that you have nothing to fear.

Answer: I believe companies should check out employees. I have worked very hard for my credentials and experience. I welcome the opportunity to have my former employers speak of me.

Chapter 9

Questions About Relationship Skills or Problems

◆

I have striven not to laugh at human actions, not to weep at them, nor to hate them, but to understand them.

—Benedict Spinoza

One question on an employer's mind is, "How will this candidate get along with my staff?" Any manager knows that if conflicts or poor relationships develop, he is the one who will have to devote a great deal of time to working through those difficulties. Managers want to avoid those worrisome and time-consuming problems. You can expect questions, perhaps cleverly disguised, like the following:

◆ Have you had personality clashes with peers in the past?

◆ Are you difficult or hard to get along with?

◆ Are you temperamental or moody?

◆ What irritates you?

◆ How will you perform under pressure?

◆ Are you a team player?

◆ Are you easygoing and flexible?

◆ Are you self-centered?

◆ Do you have unrealistic expectations of others?

◆ Do you drive others too hard?

◆ Are you too aggressive?

Be sure that you convey that you are a delight to work with under all conditions. Your answers should convey that you are a team player, flexible, and skilled at interpersonal relations.

A few of the many good words to use are *collaborative, friendly, dynamic, harmonious, cordial, synergistic, fun, warm, amiable, social, sincere, authentic, supportive, team, teamwork,* and *encouraging.*

Try to drop into the interview one or more of these phrases:

♦ on good terms with

♦ high level of trust

♦ mutually supportive

♦ stand behind

♦ highly productive

GENERAL

Keep it very positive. If the interviewer asks a second more probing question, still keep it positive. Give lots of credit to your teammates.

Question: Describe your relationships with coworkers.

Answer: We had a great group. It was one of those mixes of personalities where we truly complemented one another. I could enthusiastically support every one of them and they definitely supported me. You could describe our relationships as professional but friendly, productive but relaxed with one another.

Question: What words characterize your coworkers?

Answer: My teammates were talented, energetic, supportive, enjoyable to work with, and trustworthy. I respected and liked them.

Question: What personal qualities have helped you in your career? Contributed to your success?

Answer: People like me and they trust me. I can see when a teammate or my boss needs a little extra help and I enjoy offering it. I believe that all those things balance out eventually. My coworkers in the past have known that I am a person they can trust and depend on. And I enjoy people. I enjoy my work and I think people enjoy being around me because of that.

or

Answer: I am enthusiastic, trustworthy, and a team player. The enthusiasm I bring to the job makes working toward goals more enjoyable for me and my teammates. The high level of trust my coworkers have in me creates a real bond and helps us when we are sharing responsibilities or going through busy periods. Finally, I think that because I am first and foremost a team player, I am more productive and happier on the job. All of that has contributed to my success.

Questions:

1. With what other departments in the company do you interface? Describe those relationships. How productive are these relationships?

2. How would people in other departments describe their relationships with you?

Answer: I have really strong relationships with people in other departments, even friendships. I start out serving them as internal customers or they provide me with services, but after a while a relationship grows. I think that is because they first learn to trust me because I consistently honor my commitments and responsibilities, but what really comes through is that I like all kinds of people and enjoy having a relaxed, friendly relationship with people I work with every day.

Question: Briefly describe the people who work for you.

Answer: My team is such a great group of people. First there is Myna, who brings such energy and enthusiasm to our team. She is often the first to jump on board with a project or anything new, a real change agent. Then there is Joe, our analytical team member, who the rest of the group trusts to help them examine ideas and make sound decisions. Russ offers the team leadership among his peers and is sort of their catalyst to spur them on in tough times. Finally, there is Sue, who is the consummate listener, the thoughtful one. She is probably the strongest team member of all because she is so intuitive and insightful about relationships with customers, management, and among ourselves.

Question: What sort of people do you find most difficult?

Answer: You know, I have a different perspective on difficult people. After I had children and saw that people come into the world with such diverse personalities and even quirks, I never looked at adults the same again. I know that although some things people say or do may at first appear difficult, they probably feel they have a valid reason for responding in a particular way. I just try to figure out what they need from me and work out things to be a win-win for them and me. Of course, some people take more effort than others, but it's sometimes like solving a mystery—trying to figure out what works.

or

Answer: If I come across someone who is responding in a way that seems different or difficult, I apply what I learned in a seminar about personalities. If the person is a driver-type personality, he will respond differently than if he is an amiable type. There is no malice or intent attached; it's just a difference in style. Once you know that, you can adapt your response to his style. I think we often jump to conclusions that people are difficult when really they are just different. It's very effective.

or

Answer: Some of my best work relationships have been with people who at first seemed difficult. I've learned that my perception that someone is difficult may be triggered by the fact that I am observing them when they are under a lot of pressure or when they feel defensive or vulnerable. There are all kinds of events that can lead to a person being difficult. I look at it as problem solving. Once I can discreetly find out what is driving the problem, I can usually build a relationship with almost anyone.

Questions:

1. Describe a problem you have had with a coworker. What did you do about it?

2. What types of things have you disagreed with coworkers about in the past?

Answer: Other than minor differences of opinion over details such as what colors we should use on the annual report or where to hold a meeting, my teammates and I have really had great relationships with one another. If I did have a major problem, I would first examine the problem to see what I needed to change on my end to work it out. Second, but most important, I would try to communicate about the problem with the other person. And finally, I would end with trying to create a solution that would be advantageous for us both.

I suppose the reason we never had big problems on our team was that we all communicated all the time. Differences were welcomed and talked about instead of resented. Communication was the key.

or

Answer: Our team considered disagreement over work issues a healthy part of any project. There was such a high level of trust that a disagreement about how a project should progress was not a problem but a constructive way of examining all ways of looking at a project. We all liked each other, so we knew that we were arguing about issues, not personalities. And we *definitely* had very different personalities. We knew it and could laugh about it. I guess the laughter helped keep the disagreements friendly.

Question: Have you served in focus groups or committees? What did you contribute?

Answer: Yes, I have enjoyed helping contribute to decisions made at my current company by serving on focus groups. I was very proud of the accomplishment of one focus group in particular. We were able to examine the various healthcare vendors and advise our company about which ones would be offered to employees as possible healthcare providers. We went through very detailed information and came to a decision by our deadline. All of us contributed ideas. I represented the perspective of our departmental members from Operations. I was very proud that I could work with my teammates to accomplish this goal.

Chapter 10

Questions About Your Boss

◆

By working faithfully eight hours a day you may eventually get to be a boss and work twelve hours a day.

—Robert Frost

WORKING FOR DIFFERENT BOSSES / AUTHORITY PROBLEMS

Of immediate interest to your prospective boss is this question:

"Will this candidate respect me, work cooperatively with me, and be easy to manage—or will I regret this hire?"

A sharp interviewer will be able to uncover any problems you have had working for superiors in the past. Though you may not find it valid, interviewers do think that your past problems may be indicative of problems in the future. Be sure to portray yourself as the following:

◆ positive about former bosses

◆ appreciative of constructive feedback and past experiences

◆ complimentary of your former managers

◆ not defensive or apologetic

Even the worst boss in the world has redeeming qualities. After all, she has risen to the level above yours. Ask yourself what skills she has that have helped her get in this position. You can compliment those skills. Here are a few traits you might be able to praise in your boss if you are asked:

- ◆ working with others
- ◆ technical skill
- ◆ organizational skills
- ◆ interdepartmental support
- ◆ networking
- ◆ interpersonal skills

- ◆ industry knowledge
- ◆ seasoning and experience
- ◆ flexibility
- ◆ planning
- ◆ efficiency
- ◆ strategic thinking

Which brings up the question, "Should you lie?" The answer is No, but you are not required to confess everything you know. Advice to interviewees is much like the advice mothers give to young children.

- ◆ "If you can't say something nice, just don't say anything at all."
- ◆ "There is a little bit of good in everyone."
- ◆ "You catch more flies with honey than with vinegar."
- ◆ "Don't say anything behind someone's back you wouldn't say to her face."

This translates to:

If you can't think of something nice to say, skirt the question and say something that is very general and positive. Think of one good thing about your boss and share that. Interviewers want to see a honey-tongued candidate, not a disgruntled employee. And don't burn bridges with a former employer by bashing her. You may have had an outstanding boss and can answer all of the questions below with glowing compliments. If, however you are like most people, you may need to practice the diplomatic answers below.

GENERAL

Question: What four words best describe your boss?

Answer: My former boss was flexible, strategic, friendly, and supportive. He taught me a lot about how to adapt to constantly changing schedules and how to think strategically. Simultaneously, he was just a very friendly guy. He showed me how to build relationships with other departments by being supportive.

The above answer is a subtle code for: "My boss basically did nothing. He saved his job by knowing how to schmooze the right people. Yes, he was friendly, but not to me. He was calculating and out for himself."

Question: Describe your boss.

Answer: A really great guy. No one knew more about information systems than Robert. I was so fortunate that I was able to work for him, because he taught me all he knew, and what a great teacher. He was knowledgeable and very honest.

That answer may be code for: "This guy had the interpersonal skills of a rock. The only reason I know he was honest is that he wouldn't have the imagination to think of a lie. He knew computers and that was it."

Question: What are your manager's strengths?

Answer: Adrienne is one of the most effective people in working with others that I have ever met. She seemed to have an intuitive sense of what motivated people and how to use that for the benefit of the team. Her door was always open to us. Customers liked her, too. Her understanding and openness were definitely strengths.

The above answer might mean: "Adrienne sat around in her office and gossiped all day. She had to because she was an idiot. She knew absolutely nothing about the projects we were doing, so she really couldn't make a contribution. Instead, she just visited with people all day and drew a big salary for it."

CRITICAL OF BOSS

Question: Pretend that you have been given your former boss's job. What would you have done differently?

Answer: My former boss managed by consensus, so I really was part of the decisions she made. I would have made the same ones because, in a sense, her decisions were my decisions, too. I especially was proud of her when she made the decision to spin off some of our services to Human Resources. That took a lot of courage. Yes, I really liked the decisions she made.

Question: Is your manager more hands on or does he delegate well and encourage autonomy?

> **Caution:** If you say too much about delegation, you will sound as if he dumped all his work on you. If you say he was really hands on, you may sound as if he irritated you by looking over your shoulder all the time.

Answer: Jeff struck that delicate balance between the two. He delegated well, and I appreciated the autonomy he entrusted me with. But he would also roll up his sleeves and contribute appropriately. I remember that during the strike, Jeff even went down in the lobby and greeted customers. He was a good manager.

Question: What are your manager's weaknesses?

Remember to deny any problems or critical views of people from your past. Still, you should have a "weakness" in mind in case the interviewer presses you for one. The weakness should actually make the person look good, then, you should end by saying that though some people may see this as a fault, you secretly admired your boss for it.

Answer: If Dan had an actual weakness, I don't know it. He sometimes worked too hard trying to please everyone. It's difficult to fault him for that.

or

Answer: Weakness is not a word I would associate with George. He actually had more hidden strengths than hidden weaknesses. If I have to say one thing, I guess I would have to say that he worried too much about pleasing everyone. He tried to exceed the expectations of those above him, but he was very sensitive to his staff and their needs. I really admired him for it, to tell you the truth. Still, I guess you could call that a weakness.

Question: What are your manager's greatest barriers to success for your department?

Answer: Our department is very successful, so there really aren't any barriers we have not overcome as a team. My boss faces the same challenges of doing more with less that everyone in business should expect today—but those challenges are just part of management. It actually makes business more interesting to me, and I think my boss feels the same way.

YOUR RELATIONSHIP WITH YOUR BOSS

Question: In what ways did your boss contribute to your professional development?

> **Caution:** This is a way of trying to find out a weakness of yours. Confess something that will make you and your boss look good.

Answer: My boss was the first manager I knew who realized what a great communication tool the intranet could be. She insisted that my peers and I take an intense course in the use of our company's intranet. At first, there weren't many applications for us, but as time went on, we were all so glad that we had that training. We probably worked more effectively with the intranet than any other department.

or

Answer: Upward communication. My boss taught me to better communicate up the chain of command. I had always been skilled at communicating with my peers and my staff. Shellie taught me to open up and share more with her than I had ever done with any boss in the past. She built up my confidence and taught me what was important to communicate and what was not.

Question: Did you and your supervisor ever disagree? If so, about what?

Answer: Other than playing with ideas, we really agreed on almost everything. We both liked to bring up an idea and then have the other person make suggestions such as, "What if we did it this way? What if we changed it slightly to include thus and so?"

You might call this disagreeing, but it helped us to be innovative. I believe that there is healthy disagreement, and we had that when we were brainstorming.

Question: How has your relationship with your manager developed over time?

> **Note:** This is a sneaky way to say, "What were some problems you had to work out?"

Answer: In the beginning, Jill was just a manager to me. As time went on, however, she became a mentor to me. I realized that she was really taking time to help me become a strong manager like she is. I guess you could say the relationship just improved as time went on. I respected her almost immediately, but after working for her I admire her greatly.

Chapter 11

Questions About Work Habits

◆

Curious things, habits. People themselves never knew they had them.

—Agatha Christie

What kind of employee are you? Are you lazy? Habitually late to meetings? Messy? Disorganized? Always late with paperwork?

These are just a few of the poor work habits the following questions are designed to uncover. Make sure your answers assure the interviewer that you have none of them.

GENERAL

Question: Tell me about your work habits.

Answer: Good work habits were instilled in me long ago by my first boss. I have no problems being punctual or working hard.

Question: On a scale of 1 to 10 (1 being slow, 10 being prompt), how timely is your turnaround of paperwork, expense reports, and such?

Answer: I suppose a 9 or 10. I meet all deadlines easily.

Question: Are you able to return all phone messages and e-mails on the day they are sent?

Answer: This is a nonnegotiable issue in today's workplace. The pace is just too fast. I like to check e-mails once or twice a day to make sure I am responsive. Of course, I don't check them too frequently or I would not be as productive. But yes, I clear my e-mails at least daily.

Question: What are your current responsibilities?

Tailor your answers to the job for which you are interviewing. If the potential position is in Corporate Affairs at civic organizations, mention this.

Answer: Because I work in Environmental Services, I work with our company's lobbyists to help them understand environmental issues and how to explain our position to government bodies and lawmakers. I also do the field work the other engineers do, making sure we comply with government regulations. I communicate with probably a dozen regulatory and government agencies.

or

Answer: I do strategic planning for my department, identify internal customer needs and design products to meet those needs, as well as administer the health insurance program for more than 4,000 employees.

SCHEDULES

Unless you are very sure that the culture of the place where you are interviewing will support your quirky needs for a flexible schedule, don't mention that you want to start late or leave early. Wait until a serious offer is made before you ask questions about altering the schedule.

Questions:

1. Describe your typical workday.

2. What kind of schedule do you like?

Answer: My most productive time is in the mornings, so I like to hit it hard at that time. Afternoons, I schedule my appointments with customers and vendors. This works well for me.

or

Answer: I plan my work so that I get at least two appointments in by lunchtime. The afternoons are for work that requires greater concentration such as reports or evaluations.

Question: Do you do much business over lunch?

Answer: It depends on the customer. If that is the way the customer prefers it, I invite the customer to lunch. I enjoy working with customers.

PUNCTUALITY

Question:

Would your former teammates describe you as punctual?

Answer: Yes, although I hope they remember me for more than just being punctual. We had a great team and were very respectful of one another's time.

Question: Are you more likely to be five minutes early or five minutes late?

Answer: Being five minutes early is the only way to prevent being five minutes late. I try to plan ahead.

TIDINESS AND ORGANIZATIONAL SKILLS

Question: Are your organizational skills one of your strengths?

Answer: Yes. Organizational skills are imperative in the telecommunications industry. This is a very fast-paced work environment. If I did not stay organized daily, I could not be as successful as I am.

Question: How much importance do you attach to an orderly and attractive workplace?

Answer: I value it. Of course, other priorities require a greater investment of my time during peak hours, so I concentrate on organizing my workplace at the end of each day.

Question: Describe your desk at the end of the day.

Answer: Papers to be filed have been cleared. My computer is shut down. My In box is empty. I leave my working agenda for the following day in the middle of the desk so I can get a jump-start on it the next day.

ENERGY LEVEL AND INTEREST
Questions:

1. What parts of your job do you enjoy least?

2. What do you find boring in your job?

Avoid saying that anything is boring because this indicates burnout. If you are pressed, you can pick out a task that is done once a year and call it boring, but do not describe any daily task as boring.

Answer: Boring is not a word I use much, because just about every part of my job is important. I suppose the annual file purging could be called boring, but I find it interesting to review what I've done all year.

Question: What parts of your job do you enjoy most?

Answer: I love the customer contact. I work well with customers and I like to see the results of helping them find solutions to their needs.

or

Answer: Working with my staff to produce results. Planning to use each person's strengths to produce a synergy is one thing I do best. This collaborative approach to everything from the annual budget to accounts payable helped us reduce the penalties we were paying for late pays by 20 percent.

Question: Do you like your job?

Answer: Yes, very much. I would not take a job I didn't like. I especially like the test and measurement of productivity factors. Every day my work teaches me something new.

Question: What tasks do you hope to avoid in your next job?

Answer: I really can't think of anything I would like to avoid. Nothing comes to mind.

Question: What do you like most about being an accountant (manager, librarian)?

Answer: Seeing results and working with people. As an accountant, I make the existing systems work well for the company and improve those systems. That is very satisfying. On the other hand, working with people brings a different type of satisfaction. Working to maintain the integrity of our systems calls for building good relationships with our internal customers. I feel exhilarated by doing this successfully every day.

TIME MANAGEMENT

Question: If you experience unusually heavy demands on your time, how do you prioritize tasks?

Answer: I never lose sight of the fact that I work for the company, so I ask myself, "If I owned this company, what would I want done first?" I first establish my number one priority. Then I go to the other end of the spectrum and ask myself, "What is the least important thing on this list, or what can be deferred with no penalty to anyone?" That is my lowest priority. This establishes a sort of grid for me to plug in the other items in the order of their importance. Once I get the highest and lowest, it seems to be easier to order the rest.

Question: Do you prefer jobs that bring unexpected tasks each day or one in which you can schedule your time in advance?

Answer: I like to start with a plan knowing that I can depart from it if a more compelling need comes along. Having the plan makes me more productive and organized. Still, the success I have achieved in improving customer service is mostly due to meeting unexpected challenges professionally and with a positive approach. Flexibility is just as much a hallmark today of a successful manager as is goal setting and planning.

Question: Tell about a typical interruption to your day. How do you handle it?

Answer: My team was scheduled to meet at 9:00 A.M. to plan our strategy for the Coca-Cola account. At 8:45 A.M. I learned that we had an opportunity to bid on a large project for Wal-Mart, but bids had to be in by noon. I met my team as planned, gave them strategic direction, then appointed a team leader for the Coke account. I told them I would meet with them over lunch to review their strategy with them. I pulled one other team member out of the meeting. She and I together prepared a bid for Walmart that we submitted just before noon.

At lunch, I was really impressed with the strategic plans the team had made for the Coke account. The responsibility given to the team leader had really motivated him to encourage his peers. They did a great job. Together they fine-tuned it, and we were right on schedule. Multitasking like that is pretty much a way of life in our industry.

Question: How would you handle a respected colleague who used too much of your time talking, even though in some part, the conversation was business related.

Answer: I value my time at work and I value my relationships with my colleagues. The challenge would be to protect my time so I can get the kind of results I expect from myself while not damaging a good working relationship. First, I would do the strategic things:

◆ Say things such as, "You may not see me much for a while. I have been assigned the Xerox account so I will be pretty busy."

◆ Invite the colleague to lunch, saying, "I want to hear all about your meeting with Cubbedge. My mornings are just too busy to do much catching up. Do you have a day you are free for lunch?"

Second I would do the prosthetic things:

◆ Close my door if appropriate.

◆ Appear very busy if the colleague sticks his head in the door.

◆ Work with a headset on as if I am on the phone or on the computer.

Finally, I would address the problem directly but with sensitivity, telling about my need: "With your experience, you seem to be able to stop periodically for short breaks without losing your momentum. I am not there yet. Mornings are the time I seem to be able to best concentrate on this stuff. If I take a break, I lose my train of thought. Would you mind if we got together for coffee in my office early, before the day really gets underway? I can't seem to do mid-morning coffee breaks and be as productive as you."

Question: What distracts you from working at optimum productivity?

Answer: Actually, distractions are not a problem for me for several reasons. First, I have managed diverse employees who bring all sorts of distractions into the workplace and I have learned to roll with it. Second, years of working in a cubicle have taught me to deal with noise and other distractions. Finally, my concentration on a topic or goal allows me to tune out outside thoughts.

Chapter 12

Questions About
Job Satisfaction

◆

I have learned, in whatsoever state I am,
therewith to be content.

—Bible, Philippians 4:11

Will you be a satisfied employee or will your boss have to micro-manage you? Will you be a ray of sunlight if you are added to the department or will you rain on the group's parade? Do you bring a joy and energy to the job that is infectious and spurs others on to greater performance?

Headhunters don't want to place you with a company that will regret they hired you after you've been there a few months. Both placement people and employers are looking for good, long-term hires. They are looking for people who are focused on making a contribution and not on their own satisfaction or dissatisfaction. They also want to see that spark in your eyes that shows a passion for your work. A dream hire is someone who can't wait to get to the job each day because what he does is so exciting and he does it with excellence.

The questions that follow help answer the question, "If we hire you, will you be a happy, satisfied employee a year from now, or will you be complaining, counterproductive, and a general pain to have around?"

Once again, the interviewer will base much of her judgment on your past history. You want your answers to reflect the following:

◆ a focus on the things you liked in previous jobs

◆ high energy and uncontained joy in your work

◆ a philosophical view of hardships that minimizes them

◆ lots of positive statements

◆ letting go completely of minor problems and irritants

◆ not a hint of a tone in your voice that you were a little bit disappointed in anything

◆ enjoyment of coworkers and others in the workplace

Remember: An interview is not a confessional. You are not compelled to tell about every annoying thing you ever faced in the workplace. If it is not critical to mention it, DON'T!

GENERAL

Question: What gives you satisfaction on the job?

Start with a positive, enthusiastic answer, then follow up with specifics from your profession.

Answer: I love accounting. It's so much more than numbers and balancing and finance. Bringing my experience to an accounting problem, investigating to see what the problem really is, and coming up with solutions for management is one of the most satisfying things I do. A good accountant will learn to look for the story the numbers are really telling. That makes serving others in the organization so interesting year after year. There are always new problems, new solutions, and new stories. I love this work.

Question: In which job did you find the greatest contentment?

If at all possible, you should say your current job. Occasionally, it is quite obvious that this is not true. For example, you may have taken a job that had some unpleasant surprises, and you are trying to leave after only three months. Naturally, you should not say that the job brought you the most contentment.

Answer: My current job. The work I do is very important to the company. My department serves some of our most vital internal customers. I feel great satisfaction that I do my job so well and that it makes such a contribution to other departments and ultimately to the bottom line. The people I serve acknowledge the excellence in the way I do my job. I feel content in my work.

The above answer may bring up the question, "If you are so content, why are you leaving?" You may even be tempted to keep talking and explain that even if you are not asked. But just tell how content you are. Wait for the interviewer to ask the question about leaving. Don't bring up a tricky question like this yourself.

YOUR CURRENT POSITION
Question: Are you happy in your current job?

Answer: Yes. I am happy with my coworkers, happy with the work, happy with my performance. This has been a great job to go to each day. I feel I have made a real contribution and have done good work. That makes me happy.

Question: Are you satisfied with your current position?

Answer: I am satisfied with what I do. I love the work and the people I am privileged to work with. I am interviewing because [I am ready to take that next step / I am interested in changing to the airline industry / my company is restructuring / I want to work in biotechnology and your company is a leader / I was encouraged to interview by Don Smith in your engineering department].

Question: What has made you proudest in your present position?

You must be prepared to mention specifics. Memorize about three accomplishments so that you are always prepared to trot them out when the interviewer asks a question like this.

Answer: The growth and success in our department that I have been a part of has been a source of great pride for me. Narrowing it down to just a few will take a minute. Specifically, I think the fact that I led the team that won the National Services account was a great contribution. Increasing revenue by 23 percent last year was a proud moment. And the fact that our surveys show that my accounts rate me at 91, the highest for customer satisfaction. That makes me very proud because it means a great deal of revenue for my company.

Question: [How many seminars did you conduct / How many articles did you write / How many new customers did you sign] last year? (In other words, how energetically did you work as proven by the results?)

If you were really prolific, an exact number is impressive. If not or if you simply have no clue what the exact number is, you should try the following.

Answer: I like being [in the classroom / in front of customers / on the phones / out in the field], so I was in the classroom quite a bit. I don't remember the exact number of seminars, but I know I booked more than the average. If you need that information, I can find out for you.

Questions:

1. What could have made your last job better for you?

2. What would your last boss say was a complaint you had or changes you asked for in your last job?

Deflect. Change the focus. Pass the buck. This one is dangerous.

Answer: I didn't really have any complaints. My boss had a complaint that I helped him with, so I guess you could say I shared his complaint. He saw that when we began Casual Fridays, some of the staffers were getting way *too* casual. He asked me to help in some way. I knew that coming on too strong was not the way to go. A local department store was doing informal modeling, showing clothes for Casual Fridays. I talked my boss into having our monthly staff meeting over lunch in the store's restaurant and then staying for the informal modeling. At the end, I handed out a list of recommended styles for Casual Fridays and styles that were considered inappropriate. It worked great and it was fun.

or

Answer: It was not so much a complaint as a recommendation. I saw that we were losing out on some of the most lucrative dry cleaning business in the county because of our location. I did a business case advocating a weekly delivery service. We added it, and it added 12 percent annually to our revenues.

JOY IN THE WORK

Question: What motivates you to be successful?

Answer: The work itself and the people. I have a passion for making organizations work impeccably. At the same time, I enjoy my coworkers, my boss, and our customers. Being able to produce measurable results that make me proud of the job I do, and to do it around great people, is very motivating.

or

Answer: Measurable results and acknowledgment both motivate me. At the beginning of any project, I ask myself, "How will I know if I have done this successfully?" I set my own goals and benchmarks and then I aim consistently for those goals until I achieve them. The best part is when a coworker, my boss, or a customer notes the job well done and acknowledges it.

Make sure you mention motivators that are acceptable to the company for which you are interviewing. Most companies don't want you to say that you need constant pats on the back, so mention acknowledgment from peers and customers as in the above answers. Usually, you should not mention money as a motivator unless you are in a job that values the pursuit of money. In some jobs, the more money you make, the more money the company makes. Stock brokerage is one of those. They want money to be your motivator, so your answer should be emphatically: "Money."

Question: What parts of your job are fun?

Answer: Several parts of my job are fun. I like that first moment when I am handed a task and instantly begin planning my strategy for accomplishing my goals. I enjoy the work itself: interviewing people, putting the information together, creating a report that makes it all meaningful. Of course, the success at the end is fun. When I can say, "We did it," and know we exceeded expectations—that is a high.

Question: How did you get your promotion to ____?

Answer: Three things contributed to my being promoted. First, there is no doubt that my winning the Lockheed account meant a lot; second, I had been a consistent performer, meeting or exceeding goals on every evaluation. Finally, I worked well with people up and down the line: coworkers, my boss, customers.

or

Answer: Although there were many things that paved the road to that promotion, I think that my reputation as a problem solver really earned it for me. The job offered new challenges almost every day. Management wanted someone who would be creative in coming up with positive solutions that made good business sense. I am an innovator and had a track record for getting results. Some people think that I was promoted because I brought in 15 percent more sales than the average sales rep. Others think I got it because I have always been willing to work on committees and have made contributions that way. I just think they wanted someone who could be very effective at handling the problems that inevitably come up in this business.

DISSATISFACTION

Question: If you couldn't do this, what would you do?

Answer: I'd probably do something similar to this because I really love working in Human Resources. It's hard to imagine anything else because this is what I really want to do. I suppose I might work in accounting because I enjoy the statistical and analytical part of my job. Or I might work in sales because that would allow me to still work with people, which I enjoy, too.

Question: Have you ever considered pursuing a different career? Tell me about it.

Answer: There was a time when I was offered a position in development, and I gave it some thought. Once I really thought about what I would miss in this work, I knew I did not want to do anything else. It actually made me enjoy my job more than ever because it made me examine all I love doing and accomplishing in this position.

or

Answer: Not seriously. I have had offers and, of course, I have briefly thought about it, but I like to get results. In this job, you can see results. For example, look at last year. We had more houses completed than in any year in past history. I like to be successful and this is a field in which I can be consistently successful.

Question: What have been some of the disappointments in your career?

Either deny disappointment or admit something that is so small or that happened so long ago it can't hurt you.

Answer: I have been very fortunate in my career. I have seen steady progress and no setbacks. I realize that part of this is having worked for good companies, but I work hard and set higher goals for myself than my management sets for me. I believe I have contributed to my own good luck.

or

Answer: Although I have been rewarded for my success and have no real disappointment, I guess I just wish that I had known that I was going to enter this field when I was in college. When I first entered real estate, I went back and got an MBA in Real Estate Finance in the evenings. I wish I had majored in that in college because that would have helped in my first year or two.

Chapter 13

Questions About Honesty

◆

Tell the truth / But tell it slant.

—Emily Dickinson

No doubt about it: Honesty is the best policy. Employees with a strong ethical core are highly valued. In retail, banking, and many other industries, honesty is the number one qualification.

Of course, you want to appear honest and trustworthy, but you don't want to come off as the moral guardian of the company and your coworkers. Your boss may even become concerned that you will tell more than you should to customers or even vendors in your penchant for telling all the truth all the time. These questions identify the tricky questions related to honesty.

Question: Have you ever had any problems with an expense report?

Answer: No. I document everything and all my expenses are easily justifiable.

Question: If you travel and save the company money, do you think it's ever permissible to pocket some of the savings?

Answer: Never. Everyone is charged with the responsibility to save the company money in whatever way we see. It is the company's money. We all have a vested interest in keeping expenses down.

Question: Is cheating or theft grounds for dismissal?

> *Your stand should be that cheating and theft are wrong without sounding rigid and condemning.*

Answer: Yes. In every case I can think of the answer would be Yes. I suppose if you are talking about walking out with paper clips, there might be other interventions, but in my experience, the answer is Yes.

Question: Do you think an employee should volunteer information to the boss if another employee is committing petty thefts?

Answer: I can't imagine looking over a coworker's shoulder to the degree that I would even know that. If it were that blatant, I would go to my boss. If it were that blatant, however, I think the boss would already know.

Question: Do you think honesty is always the best policy?

This is often asked of sales professionals. How much of your product's weakness will you tell customers? How much of your secret weapons for closing a deal would you disclose to competitors?

If you are interviewing for most companies, the answer is a simple and enthusiastic, "Yes, honesty is the best policy." If you think a sales manager may be concerned about your telling too much, you might try the following.

Answer: When my mother asks me if she looks as if she has gained weight, honesty is *not* the best policy. In every work situation, however, honesty *is* the best policy. Being honest does not mean that you have to tell every detail of what you know to those outside the company, though. I do believe in honoring my employer's desire for confidentiality.

Question: In what situations might it be acceptable to stretch the truth in order to sell a product (or satisfy regulators or inspectors)?

Answer: I don't believe it's stretching the truth so much as not telling everything you know. We are all out there trying to present our products in the best light. The customer knows this. I think we confuse customers by telling them too much. If they have concerns and they ask, I believe you should be honest with them. I don't believe in bringing up problems and concerns that might not ever arise. That is not representing my company well.

Question: How do you feel about confidentiality agreements?

Answer: No problem. An employer has a right to ask for loyalty.

Question: Have you ever been placed in an ethical dilemma on the job? Tell me about it.

Answer: No. I am fortunate to have always worked for great companies and great people. I think when you work with people who think as you do, these dilemmas don't tend to arise. That's one reason that I am interested in this company.

Chapter 14

Questions About Balance: Hard Worker or Burnout Candidate?

◆

If you want creative workers, give them enough time to play.

—John Cleese

WORKAHOLICS

Question: How do you feel about workaholics?

Be sure to start with a statement about your own strong work ethic. Do not, however, call yourself a workaholic. Also, be sure to make your leisure activities sound vivid and fun. Be specific. If you realize you haven't done anything fun in a while, go do something. You'll perform better in the interview.

Answer: I have a very strong work ethic myself, so it's hard for me to find too much fault if you are talking about employees who simply work very hard. But if you are talking about true workaholics who work very hard for a while, then run out of steam or experience other work-related problems because they have not maintained balance, that's different. Then I would say I feel about them as I feel about anyone who has a performance problem. I would offer them my support in a nonjudgmental way and help them work through the problem.

Question: Would anyone in your past describe you as a workaholic?

Answer: I do bring a lot of energy to the work, so I guess that is possible. I love this work and get really into it. I also understand that because we deal with [utilities / sales / entertainment / food], some long hours are required. I don't call that being a workaholic;

I call that being a professional. What saves me from becoming a workaholic is my passion for waterskiing and my time with my family. No matter how busy I am, I take time out to enjoy myself. I think that balance refreshes me for upcoming work.

or

Answer: Anyone who gets into this industry and expects to work strictly nine to five would probably think I am a workaholic. Professionals at my level know that there are times that long hours are required. What is important is to maintain balance. My leisure time is important to me, too. My wife and I take frequent walks on a nature trail near our home. We also take fun vacations that we enjoy planning. I guess you could say that although I like to work hard, I like to play hard, too.

WEAK WORK ETHIC

Question: Has anyone ever mistakenly felt that he was doing more than his share of a team project with you?

Answer: No. I am a team player. My parents instilled in me a strong work ethic. If I saw that someone was struggling to do his share, I'd pitch in and help.

Question: On a scale of 1 to 10—10 being a workaholic and 1 being too laid back—where would you put yourself on the scale?

> **Note:** First define workaholic.

Answer: Although I really enjoy the job and work hard at it, I do try to maintain balance. To me, a true workaholic misses the satisfaction of being a team player and can't collaborate, so I guess I shouldn't place myself at a 10. I guess I'll say an 8 for working hard but not crossing that line into the burnout experienced by people who haven't learned how to lead a balanced life.

PRESSURE

Question: What do you do when you realize you are getting behind in your work?

Answer: I prioritize first. Often, I find that some of the tasks on my desk are not time critical, so I can move them to the bottom of my To Do list. Second, I look at my resources. If I am spending time doing things that a staff member or a secretary can do, then delegating would probably be good for me and developmental for them. Of course, there are those times that simply putting in a few extra hours or taking paperwork home is necessary.

Question: What sorts of things frustrate you? Make you impatient?

> **Note:** Choose an answer that makes you look excited and not frustrated. Pick a technology, seasonal happening, or event in your industry and say how excited you become about it. This puts a whole new slant on impatience.

TECHNICAL

Answer: I get really excited about new software when its introduction has been announced. I guess I get impatient because I can't wait to learn it and then use it to make ourselves more efficient.

SALES

Answer: The only frustrating thing about sales in this industry is that there are just so many opportunities. I have become adept at focusing on those opportunities that offer the greatest potential rewards for both me and the company. If that is a problem, then I think it's a great one to have.

ENJOYING THE WORK
Questions:

1. What is fun to you? (See Chapter 12, p. 95.)

2. What do you find challenging?

Do not, under any circumstances, say that a critical part of your job is difficult. Choose instead to state that the only real challenges are those higher-than-expected goals that you set for yourself.

Answer: I set new challenges for myself all the time. Mastering the tactical and the technical skills of my job was accomplished long ago. Now, I challenge myself by doing this job more efficiently each year and by achieving increasingly better numbers. The innovations I bring to this job make it more fun for me. For example, I used to spend a great deal of time sending out information. Before the department was fully using the Internet, I set up a simple web site where customers could get preliminary information on our products. Our technical customers especially loved it. That application saved me several hours each month. I used that time to solve more serious customer service problems. We ended last year with the fewest files on our trouble desk than we have ever had.

SALES
Answer: A real sales professional is in essence self-motivated. You either have that love of posting higher and higher numbers or you don't. That is what challenges me. I don't want to just beat the competition; I want to beat my own personal best. Now *that's* a challenge. I also am open to new ways to sell and to learning to incorporate new strategies and new products into what is already succeeding for me.

TECHNICAL
Answer: I love the way this industry is constantly changing. We are in an explosive growth period of new ideas, new technology, and new information. That challenge makes coming to work every day really interesting and attractive. That's one of the reasons I chose this profession.

Question: What are you doing to achieve your goals?

Answer: Twice a year, I assess my job and set goals for myself. These are in addition to the goals set for me by my manager. Then I identify two or three things I will do to help me achieve these goals. For example, right now I am taking a finance course in order to deal with customers in the financial side of the business.

or

Answer: One of my goals is to become more experienced working with larger accounts so I will be more versatile. I am working with one of the National Accounts reps to become a strong force in that part of our business. Although I work with National Accounts only occasionally, I believe that this peer training will help me be more effective with these extremely valuable customers.

TEAM BALANCE

Question: What have you had to give up for your career—or for any job in the past?

Answer: I can't say that I have given anything up. Of course I have enjoyed the people I've worked with in every position, and moving up as I have means leaving good colleagues behind, but I don't look at that as giving something up.

SALES MANAGEMENT

Answer: If you mean do I miss sales, then I guess the answer is Yes and No. I still go out on selected calls with my team, both for their development and to build executive relationships with those companies. In that sense, I haven't given up sales. But I always enjoyed the strategic part of selling: planning the calls and bulletproofing presentations. I still get to do that with my staff. In fact, I get to share some of the winning strategies that worked for me. I enjoy that as much as sales.

Question: Are you usually the hardest-working member of your team?

Answer: Every team I have ever served on has had other hardworking members in addition to me, but I would be considered one of the hardest-working members. I think if you have good relationships, people tend to want to pull together to accomplish goals. I do like to approach my work with a lot of energy toward achieving goals, but I really am not looking at it in terms of "Am I working harder?" I just love [trading / selling / designing / hospital administration].

POTENTIAL JOB LONGEVITY? STEPPING-STONE MOVE?

Question: Would you leave a job for slightly more money?

Answer: No. If you chase the money only, you don't have time to make the really big contributions to any one company. It has been by getting to know a company and achieving results in that company that I have been able to achieve the results that I have. I could do this only by investing all my energy in the company that employed me.

Questions:

1. Would you describe yourself as ambitious?

2. How important are promotions to your long-range plan?

The hidden danger here is that in some industries, management layers are being trimmed away and promotions are few and far between. If you are applying for a position that offers no hope of promotion for years, you don't want to sound too confident that you will move up the ladder. The interviewer may fear that you will become dissatisfied once you see the lack of opportunity.

On the other hand, some companies want to see that you have a desire to grow and to move up through their ranks. They want to hear a confident person who desires growth.

You must do your research about this company and this position. Into which of the above categories does this job fit?

The first answer is for a position that offers little opportunity for promotions.

The second answer is for a position with a company that is looking for ambitious, promotable employees.

Answer: Of course, any really long-range plan would include an eventual promotion. I have always been successful; I will continue to be successful, and eventually that means a promotion. But I also am a student of the business. In our industry, promotions are not as frequent as they once were. I think I have a confident but realistic perception about my future promotions.

or

Answer: Professional growth is one of my goals. I plan to be successful and that will mean handling more responsibility and upward movement. One reason I want to work for XYZ Company is that I can build a career here because of the great opportunity you offer. I look forward to doing whatever it takes to follow a successful career path to even better positions, in time.

Questions:

How have you felt rewarded in previous jobs?

Answer: Completing a project that has met the expectations of clients and management and still comes in under budget and on time is satisfying to me. Knowing that I have contributed to the development of my staff members while simultaneously getting them to give their best to the company is satisfying. The awards such as the Production Award and the industry awards I have received are, of course, satisfying, but it's the consistent day-to-day achievements that really are the most satisfying to me.

SATISFACTION IN SALES

Answer: Setting new benchmarks in sales is what I find satisfying. I am not satisfied with just meeting goals; I like to post numbers that I have not reached before. Selling more than 200 policies in my first year at Provident was satisfying. I also like customer care. I like my customers and they like me.

Chapter 15

Questions About Money

◆

Keep cool and collect.

—Mae West

And now comes the thorny money questions. Following are some of the thoughts going through a candidate's mind when the interviewer starts to ask questions related to salary and compensation:

◆ Am I pricing myself out of the market?

◆ Will the salary I state be too low and raise doubts about my value?

◆ Am I settling for too little? Would they have paid more?

◆ Do I appear unsophisticated, greedy, and unmotivated (or a host of other fears)?

There are times when you know an exact amount or salary range to state and can name that dollar amount confidently. At other times, you may have concerns that you are saying the wrong thing. For those iffy moments, the answers below can be adapted to your use. Don't forget the following, however.

CARDINAL RULE OF SALARY NEGOTIATIONS

> *Get the Employer to Name a Number First!*

Although this is not always possible, it is always preferable. Also, try not to mention salary until the end of the interview, when an offer is on the table.

PERFORMANCE PAY, COMMISSIONS, INCENTIVES

Question: Do you think performance should be rewarded over experience?

Again, do your homework. If you know that a company always promotes based on experience, choose experience. If this employer wants to reward the top producers, choose performance. If you don't know, choose the answer below.

Answer: I have always been a top performer, so naturally I find pay for performance appealing. Experience counts, too, however. One way a person learns to be a top producer is through experience. I have always been well compensated in my jobs because I produce results. I think that anyone who consistently performs a job with excellence and is committed to a company will eventually be rewarded.

Question: How do you feel about performance incentives?

Answer: Because I am a very self-motivated top performer, I like the idea of performance incentives. They are like the icing on the cake. Producing consistent results, however, is more a matter of talent and your own drive. The performance pay is just a bonus. That real drive I have had to be the leader in productivity results for three consecutive quarters has come from within.

Question: How would you like to be compensated?

Do your research. If performance pay or commission is their method of compensation, be sure to include that in your answer. If you have a definite compensation plan in mind and don't feel it is risky asking for it directly, go for it. You run no risk if you know they will give it to you, or you don't care if you get the job or not and have nothing to lose by asking.

Answer: In addition to salary, I look for incentive in terms of performance pay, bonuses, or appropriate raises. I am a proven manager and want to join a company that will compensate me in some way after I have proven myself valuable. What did you have in mind?

> **Note:** If you know this is a salary-only job, use the following answer.

Answer: With an established company like yours, salaries are usually commensurate with a person's abilities and experience. What did you have in mind?

> **Note:** Both answers above end by putting the interviewer on the spot to disclose the compensation package.

Question: This job pays a small base plus commission. (SILENCE)

Answer: That was what I was hoping. Commission rewards sales professionals, which I am. I expect to be one of your top producers. What are those people, as well as your first-year people, earning?

SALARY

Question: What are your salary expectations?

(See the second answer on page 123.)

Question: What sort of salary are you looking for?

Answer: I am sure that Rockwell International compensates employees as well as others in this industry. What kind of a range will this position offer?

or

Answer: In my last job, I earned $73,000 a year. Of course, part of my incentive to leave that job is to improve that. Am I correct in assuming that this position would offer me that salary increase, and, if so, what is your range?

or

Answer: You are one of the first companies I have interviewed with, so I am still getting a feel for the market. I will say that I chose to interview here first because I am very interested in working for you. If the salary were attractive, I would have no problem making a commitment. Can you tell me the range?

Questions:

1. What would it take to bring you on board?

2. What is your range as far as salaries go?

If you have a definite salary in mind and your research makes you confident you will not be either selling yourself short or pricing yourself out of the market, state the amount. Also, don't forget to negotiate for telecommuting, health benefits, 401(K), and other benefits at the appropriate time, after a firm offer is on the table.

Answer: I would have to understand all the possibilities for rewards in your company: Are there bonuses or incentives? Is there opportunity for growth and promotion? What are the benefits? Is there a matching program for my 401(K) plan? I look at a lot in addition to salary. If there are many options for being rewarded I could see my range being anywhere from 50 to 65 a year. What is the range of this position and what about any other types of compensation?

Question: How do you formulate your salary expectations?

Answer: I know I have a lot to offer as a manager and as a professional in this industry. I look at many things in addition to salary to see a total compensation package: Are there bonuses or incentives? Is there opportunity for growth and promotion? What are the benefits? Is there a matching program for my 401(K) plan? All that will be taken into consideration when I receive an offer. What does Equifax offer in terms of this position?

HIGHER/LOWER SALARY

Question: This salary is [lower than / not a step up from] your last position. How do you justify this lack of growth in your income?

Answer: I am making this move in order to move to the technology sector. I consider that an advance in my career and I am willing to take a chance that this will be a great move for me personally and professionally. I have long-term career goals to achieve and this move fits right in.

Other acceptable answers to the above are as follows.

◆ to break into management, academics, or some other area of expertise

◆ to make the move to a Fortune 500 company

◆ to be a part of the innovative work being done at Searle (or other company)

◆ to be a part of the work you do for NASA (or other exciting project)

◆ to work closer to home

◆ to stop traveling (Be very sure there is no travel with this job.)

Question: This salary is substantially higher than your last salary. What qualifies you to make such a great leap?

Answer: That is why I am interviewing. I am ready for this. Even my current management knows that I am ready for this, but they are in a salary freeze and can't promote anyone for quite some time. This salary is actually where I would normally be if the freeze had not been instituted.

or

Answer: I have recently completed my MBA degree. I am now in a different place in the market.

or

Answer: I have really not done a competitive search of the market in years. I love the company I work for even though I am aware that they are notorious in the industry for being on the low end of the pay scale. I have learned so much and enjoyed the work, so I just haven't been motivated to make the move until recently. I have been approached by a few headhunters with jobs that pay quite a bit more, but I thought that I would first interview here since this is where I'd really like to work. Wherever I go, the pay will be better.

or

Answer: The success I have achieved in [quality control / sales / operations] can be transferred to other [industries / companies / departments] that offer higher compensation. I produce strong results in improving quality control and companies to whom quality control is a priority pay more for it.

Chapter 16

Questions About Mistakes and Problems

◆

Experience is the name everyone gives to their mistakes.

—Oscar Wilde

An experienced interviewer is trained to sniff out problems. If there is any hidden problem, the following questions are designed to bring it into the open. Some of the things the interviewer is fishing for include

◆ mistakes you have made.

◆ attitude problems.

◆ poor judgment.

◆ a difficult or whiney personality.

◆ unrealistic expectations.

◆ ruthlessness or aggression.

Adapt the answers below to your background and your profession.

MISTAKES

Question: Given the gift of hindsight, what would you do differently in your career?

Do not sound dissatisfied and whiney. Turn this into a pat on the back for you. Start with a statement that sounds as if you have no regrets because, after all, you are a success. Then admit something that could in no way hurt you and could possibly help you.

Answer: It's amazing how one never really wastes any experience or education. I think everything I ever did contributes to the success I enjoy today. Maybe I should have gotten into this [industry / profession / company] sooner because I love it. But if I had, maybe I wouldn't have the satisfaction and success I enjoy today.

Question: Tell me about the biggest mistake you ever made on the job. How did you handle it?

Answer: Mistake. . . . I can't think of a really big mistake. Years ago, I was working on a report for my boss. I was concentrating so hard on the content that I forgot to back up as I went. It was a major report and I had been composing it all day. My computer chose that day to crash. I had to recreate about half of it. I stayed up until 2:00 A.M. You only need that to happen to you once to learn that lesson.

The above answer has been sanitized in the following ways:

◆ You have distanced yourself with time. This happened "years ago."

◆ You have absolved yourself by "learning that lesson."

◆ Your mistake was not a reflection on your skills, professionalism, or anything really important. This is a small mistake.

◆ You made it right by coming through for your boss.

EXPECTATIONS

Question: What working conditions do you prefer?

If this is an office job, say that you enjoy the office environment. If the position requires you to be out on appointments all day, say that you are energized by that. Do your homework and tailor your answer to this job. If you are not sure, try the following answer.

Answer: I have worked in an office and on the road doing appointments all day. Either one can be energizing. I am really not focused on the conditions around me but on the work. I guess you could say that I don't have a preference about the conditions as long as I am working in [my area of expertise / accounting / operations].

Question: Every job has problems. What are some problems that are part of your current job?

Answer: Problem solving is one of the most intriguing parts of my job. When a customer or a staff member comes to me with a problem, I try to come up with a solution that is satisfying to everyone. To me, it's like solving a puzzle, which I find deeply satisfying. Our problems are minor, anyway. They primarily relate to shipments being late or lost. These are fairly easy to deal with quickly and to everyone's satisfaction.

or

Answer: Our problems are just the business-as-usual problems that are part of this industry: rush orders or emergency shipments. I have great relationships with other departments and our vendors, so these really don't even seem like problems to me.

Answer for Executives: The problems of the job are just the problems of the industry. [Airlines will always be looking for better technology to deal with weather and scheduling. / Food suppliers will always be looking for better storage and delivery methods. / Marketing people will always be challenging themselves to find more intriguing media and untapped markets.] In my job I am like an explorer finding new paths to successfully offer solutions for my staff to implement. I need to be open and teachable regarding innovations in this industry that can help us solve these problems better, faster, and at a lower cost.

PROBLEMS

Question: In what areas would you like to improve?

Mention some wonderful developmental step that you are taking that is so far beyond your manager's expectations that it makes you look good. Such things as speedreading and learning Chinese turn this question aimed at negatives into a boost for you. Do not mention anything you are doing to fix a weakness because you don't want to confess to weaknesses in the interview.

Answer: I am reading a book on learning styles that I believe will help me manage my staff more effectively. You know, today we are expecting our people to learn, adapt, and take in a great deal of information at a very fast pace. Learning how the people I work with daily take in information best will help me help *them* perform better. We will all be more successful that way.

or

Answer: I am a lifelong learner, so improvement is something I strive to do every day. By setting higher goals for myself than my manager sets for me, I am able to improve my productivity. It's a challenge I set for myself personally and I enjoy the pace.

or

Answer: I am learning to compartmentalize what I do better. Focusing on just one thing at a time is difficult for a busy [manager / sales rep / insurance agent]. I want to give the people that I interface with on the job, whether staff or peers, the feeling that they are the only person on the floor or in my mind.

Question: Would you say you are an overachiever or underachiever?

Be sure to say first that you don't fall into either category because you are successful. Then proceed to tell how you excel in both areas. Turn it into a positive. All the time, assure the interviewer that you are trying to cooperate and answer the question.

Answer: I am an achiever, so I guess that is a natural question. I honestly believe I have used my gifts and abilities well. In the sense that I know I am in the most productive phase in my career and that the best is best to come, I guess you can say that I have not achieved in the past what I am capable of in the future. In that sense, I am an underachiever. But my final answer would be overachiever in the sense that given the resources I have had in the past, I have achieved well beyond the expectations of senior management.

Question: What changes would you make if you came on board?

If you know that the company wants to hire you because you can put their records on DVD, then by all means the answer should be,

"Put the records on DVD." But you may not know what the company wants.

◆ Do they want immediate results and change?

◆ Are they skeptical of a new person making radical changes?

◆ Do they fear that change will cost them too much?

If you have done your research on this department and position, you may know the specific answer they are looking for. If not, try the following:

Answer: I would find out what changes senior management wants to see. I would talk to staff members and peers from other departments for their ideas about changes. Above all, I'd informally survey the people we serve to find out if changes are needed. After reviewing budgets and other resources, I would create a strategic plan, gain approval, and then begin to implement change.

or

Answer: I make decisions by consensus, so all changes would be a collaborative effort with peers, management, and staff. Change is an inevitable part of constantly improving our processes, but it needs to be intelligent change. I have some great experience that gives me ideas of my own, but I want to draw ideas from my coworkers, too.

Question: Has your advancement been commensurate with your abilities?

Be careful here. You are probably applying for a job that means advancement so your present job is not commensurate with your abilities. Be very relaxed about saying that you are ready for advancement now, and you are very happy with your present company and boss.

Answer: Well, of course, I am ready for a move now, but overall I think it has been. If I did not move as quickly through the ranks when I was younger, it was not because of my abilities. I just wasn't savvy about career moves, strategically approaching the job market, or packaging myself through résumés and other job-search methods. As far as my work went, I could probably have moved up faster, but learning to manage my career took me a bit of time.

or

Answer: I suppose we all have felt competent to move on and had to wait for opportunities, but overall I have been pleased with the direction of my career. I really enjoy my current job. I am just ready for more responsibility.

or

Answer: Although I love my present company and the people with whom I work, I am ready to move up. Despite the fact that I enjoy [making the contributions I am making / making the big sales / leading the company in production], I need to go where the opportunities are.

It is acceptable to say no to this question if you were finishing a degree or if there were a positive, logical reason for your being held back that could never be a problem ever again. For example, once you have a degree, you have it, so that could not be a problem to this employer, which is his concern.

Answer: In my early career, I was held back by not having a degree, which is a must today. I simply attended school at night until I solved that problem. And, of course, I am ready to advance now.

Chapter 17

Questions About Performance

◆

It is better to wear out than to rust out.
—Richard Cumberland

Every employer wants top performance from a new hire. Look for ways to describe yourself in terms such as the following.

◆ producer

◆ high energy

◆ performance-driven

◆ get results

◆ high achiever

◆ consistent performer

◆ lead the company in . . .

◆ proactive

◆ showed initiative in . . .

PAST PERFORMANCE

Question: Describe your performance in your past position.

Answer: I consistently produced results in [inventory control improvement / sales / productivity / customer satisfaction]. My performance was outstanding in other areas as well. For example, I put together the first program for getting on-line bids for our department that cut costs by 8 percent and [cite another example from your background]. I have a long history of excellent performance.

or

Answer: I am a high-energy person, so performance is an area in which I excel. I also try to work smart, so that I get the most from myself and others without wasting time in nonproductive activities. I produced more outdoor sign sales than any other sales manager in the region [or other example]. I also had the lowest absenteeism level in my department of any manager in our region [or other example].

Question: Were you pleased with your performance in your last job (current job)?

Answer: Yes. I put all my energies into whatever project I am working on at the time. This focus plus my belief in planning my work and working my plan have produced great results for Johnson & Johnson. For example, I have the lowest percentage of rework and operator errors in my department of any of my peers. I won the Outstanding Manager of the Year award in my first year in Chicago. It is always satisfying to look back on the year and see how I have performed.

PERFORMANCE EVALUATIONS

Question: On a scale of 1 to 10—1 being low and 10 being high—how would your last manager rate your performance?

Answer: 10. I achieved or surpassed all my goals. My manager once told me that I was his most consistent performer. It was because of his recommendation that I got my last promotion. I perform at the 10 level because I don't just strive for the minimum.

I set stretch goals for myself, so I outperform goals set for me by others.

or

Answer: 10. Whether you measure it by results or quality or efficiency, my manager would tell you that I am easily a 10. I did things such as create a schedule that cut our overtime hours by 12 percent. That saved the company close to $5,000 a year [or cite another example]. Going beyond the status quo made my performance highly rated.

or

Answer: High ratings such as a 10 are what I am used to. Throughout my career, my performance evaluations have always included the fact that I meet or exceed my goals. I strive for my own personal best, which is usually beyond my manager's expectations. For example, last year my team logged in more than 200,000 telemarketing calls. That was 10 percent over the goal set for us. In terms of what that did for the company, it added or retained many customers. That type of drive to always better my own performance makes me a 10 in every area.

Question: Tell me about the worst performance evaluation you ever received.

Deny that you have had a bad one unless you know *positively*, *absolutely* that you have one and that the interviewer knows about it. You should never lie, but you are not obligated to tell all.

Answer: There isn't a really bad one. I have been fortunate to have had great bosses who have appreciated my performance and rated me accordingly. Of course, when I started out, a manager might have recommended training in an area to help me develop, such as in product knowledge. But those were not bad evaluations of my performance.

or

Answer: I have been rated highly throughout my career. I believe that if a professional allies himself with a credible organization like my last company or like yours, his evaluations will be fair and reflect his accomplishments. I am a high achiever and have accomplished a lot. Accomplishments such as creating the new Customer Call Center have led me to be nominated for the Leadership Development Program. My high-energy performance has also contributed to consistently high performance evaluations.

What if you were fired from your last job for poor performance and the interviewer knows it? This is so rare that it almost never happens. Be sure that the interviewer knows for sure that you were rated poorly before you even think about using an answer like the following.

Answer: Although I personally performed well, I was disappointed in my last performance evaluation. I had outperformed the market impressively, but could not completely compensate for [the downturn in the market / the disaster in our South American plants / the media disaster / the prolonged drought / the effects of the lawsuit]. Even though every performance evaluation I had ever received had been stellar, this one rocked me. I have spent a lot of time reviewing my performance and decisions I made. I am very proud of both. Still, hindsight is 20/20. Now I see things I could have possibly done differently. I think I am a much better [manager / sales rep / writer / trainer] for having experienced this. This type of seasoning is valuable in my professional development even if it was difficult for me.

Question: How were you evaluated?

If you received a good evaluation say something like the following.

Answer: Performance, achievement, results. If you had them, you received a top evaluation, as I did. Everything from numbers to staff and stakeholder feedback was taken into consideration. I know that this is a very high evaluation, but it is a valid one.

If you received a poor evaluation say something like the following.

Answer: It was subjective. There was a guide for the manager to follow, but ultimately it was a matter of his take on the situation.

or

Answer: There was a formula that my boss had to go by that was not reflective of the projects we did. It could not measure or evaluate our type of performance, but my boss was obligated to use it anyway. He would be the first to tell you that my performance was superior to what the evaluation reflects. He wanted to find some way to account for the successes I had had in salvaging more than 30 major accounts and in increasing business from chain accounts by more than 10 percent, but the assessment tool could not accommodate that. He was frustrated by it and, of course, so was I. Changes and improvements in the assessment tool are now being discussed based on what happened in our department and several others. I guess you need to look at this evaluation in the context of every other evaluation in my career to get an accurate picture. My evaluations have always been off the charts. This was just one unfortunate occurrence.

Question: What did you agree with on your performance evaluation? Disagree?

Answer: I agreed with the high ratings I received because I know I earned them. There really isn't anything in there to disagree with, because it is all strong.

or

Answer: I am proud of my high ratings and feel I earned them. Being rated superior in every category reflects the commitment that I have to excellence in this profession. I wholeheartedly agree with everything.

If you are interviewing internally and you know that your interviewer has a copy of your less-than-complimentary performance evaluation, you may want to try a different approach. Be very sure, however, that the interviewer knows your weaknesses before you confess anything. And before you confess to anything, spend a lot of time elaborating on the accomplishments that brought you one or two high marks.

Answer: I was delighted to be acknowledged for my work habits and initiative. My successful design of the new nonsmoking policy and my perfect record of completing the management reports by deadline each month were among dozens of things that contributed to these high ratings. Even though my manager and I looked at our audience differently for the reports, which contributed to my performance score not being as high as it has always been in the past, I really see this as a one-time glitch. Two professionals can look at the same information and see it differently. My performance is one of my strongest assets as all previous evaluations will attest. That is just a temporary departure.

Note how the answer handles this negative and touchy area because it

◆ impresses the interviewer first with specific examples of achievements. Very credible.

◆ describes the disagreement as seeing things differently and not as a disagreement.

◆ does not come off as disgruntled or resentful.

◆ puts this low evaluation in the context of a parade of positive evaluations.

FUTURE

Question: What contributions do you think you could make to our department?

If your research has told you that the employer is looking for someone who can do something specific such as train the sales force to present from laptops, then say, "I am the most qualified person to teach your sales force to be more effective by presenting from laptops." However, if you have no idea if the company is willing to invest in laptops, don't say that. Here is a sample answer to adapt to your industry and your background.

Answer: The same project management skills I brought to the establishment of the Atlanta office could be applied here for Meineke. I am a strong producer myself and with my collaborative management style I get remarkable results from others. I would like to apply that to helping you increase your sales volume, particularly in your high end products. My track record of steadily increasing sales in every year I was with Byers demonstrates that I can contribute sales expertise and experience. One unique thing I bring to this position is [my foreign language skills / my computer abilities / my relationship skills / my West Coast experience]. I can converse with many of the global customers whose first language is not English. That is an asset.

Chapter 18

Questions About
Meeting of
the Minds

◆

Nothing in life is to be feared. It is only to be understood.

—Marie Curie

Do you and the employer see things the same way? Are you looking at the work, the goals, and the primary duties the same way? Answering the following questions well will assure the interviewer that you are the perfect fit for this position.

FUNCTIONS AND DUTIES
Questions:

1. What would you say are the most important functions of this [job / department]?

2. Prioritize for me the duties of this position.

Before the interview, find out as much as you can about this position and what the employer's priorities are. If the job has been in the paper or has been posted, carefully review the job description and tailor answers to it. More important, listen carefully at the beginning of the interview. You may be given clues about what is important in this position and what is not.

You will have the best advantage if you know someone in the department who can tell you what the hiring manager's hot buttons are. If a Human Resources professional or placement person is presenting you as a candidate to the employer, you should also call them ahead of time and ask for a job description, if you have not already been given one.

Being prepared helps with this and many other questions.

Answer: Naturally, I would have to work with my manager to confirm what the priorities are, but going in I project that the first priority is delivery of systems to customers on a timely basis, then fiscal management and control. Keeping the executive level apprised of opportunities and risks is also an important responsibility. (Substitute where relevant the duties related to the position in question.)

SALES
Answer: Securing sales and increasing revenue is my top priority. Developing and maintaining relationships with customers, coworkers, and management is crucial to success in this role, so I would invest whatever it took to meet those needs. That would include phone calls, follow-up letters or e-mails, and meetings. Finally, being a student of the business and a good steward of the com-

pany's money and other resources is important. That could mean anything from keeping good records to negotiating better contracts.

TECHNICAL

If the answer is to surf the Net all day, then just say that. Most professional jobs, however, want you to interpret, innovate, extrapolate, and apply what you know. Employers are usually looking for a more proactive answer from a professional.

Answer: In addition to conducting tests for various bacteria, I would consider a priority of my job to communicate with the technicians. I would also find it important to apply quality control measures because mistakes can be costly. Finally, taking the initiative to make recommendations about the technology, the lab, and the processes we use would be a third responsibility. To do this I would continue to stay current in my field to look for ways to do our job better, and with greater efficiency.

YOUR QUALIFICATIONS

Tailor your answer to the employer's top priorities. You have so much in your background. Be sure to lead with experience and skills that are specifically mentioned as priorities in this position.

Questions:

1. Why do you think you are the best candidate for this position?

2. What uniquely qualifies you for this job?

Answer: I am uniquely qualified because of my outstanding performance in [presenting to executives / creating menu-style benefits packages]. My expertise in [financial sales / cost management] is stellar. Finally, the track record I have in [increasing revenues through existing accounts / managing diverse personnel at offsite locations] is exceptional, as evidenced by the achievements I had in this area with [Smith Barney / Hewlett-Packard].

DESIRE AND COMMITMENT

Always state that you are very interested before asking for more information. You would not be wasting your time in an interview if there were not some interest.

Question: How interested are you in this position?

Answer: Seriously interested. From what you have told me, I am uniquely qualified for this position. From my point of view it's a good fit. What is your take on it?

or

Answer: Extremely interested. Of course, I would like to know more about the position. Can you tell me more?

or

Answer: Working for Sony is something I very much want to do. Can you give me more information on this position so we can pursue this further?

Question: What do you want to ask me? (See Chapter 3.)

Question: Name one barrier to your saying yes to this position today.

If there is no barrier, say so immediately. If there is a problem with their offer, however, you need to be candid but very positive, friendly, and professional about it. Here are some options for responding when the perfect offer has not been put on the table.

Answer: There are more things I like about the offer than things I don't. In fact, the only thing I see that we need to work out is the compensation. Since it is not in my range, what are your options as far as supplementing it with a signing bonus or negotiating it a little higher? Everything else seems to be a great fit.

or

Answer: This is the job I want. I am willing to accept the two-week vacation instead of the three I had at Dell. The barrier for me is still that I need to telecommute at least two hours a day. What can you do to make this work?

or

Answer: The job offer sounds very good. I am especially pleased that you are agreeing to pay for the annual professional development conference I mentioned. That will help me achieve a higher level of performance by keeping our department current with technology.

The above answers are for times when a detailed offer is on the table. If there is no specific offer on the table, you have nothing to lose by saying yes, contingent on the particulars of the offer.

Answer: I see no barriers. In fact, this is pretty exciting because I very much want to work for you and this is a position in which I could make some outstanding contributions. I would really like to look at an offer if that is where you are heading.

Chapter 19

Questions About Experience

◆

Experience is not what happens to you; it is what you do with what happens to you.

—Aldous Huxley

Question: Your experience with [telecommunications / sales / information systems / lasers] is not recent. How will you compensate for this?

Answer: Every company is different and every company's technology is different. There is always a learning curve. I am adept at picking up information quickly. Plus, I am willing to devote the time. Actually, I am looking forward to it.

or

Answer: In any new job there is a great deal of information to assimilate in the first year. I have prepared myself for that. Actually, I have been doing some training on my own with a friend who is in this business. I have also kept up through conferences and the Internet. In a short time, I will be fully functioning in this position.

or

Answer: I am willing to do anything it takes to get up to speed quickly. Naturally, there is a learning curve for any new employee. If you or my peers have any suggestions for me, I invite them. I expect to invest a great deal of time in learning the job on my own, however.

Question: Tell me about your experience.

Answer: Some of my achievements include cutting the Kennestone budget by 4 percent when hospital costs were going up and managing a successful merger. I have worked in both large and midsize hospitals and have a track record for leaving each institution more profitable than when I arrived.

I have worked in this field [for 14 years / for my entire career / since college]. I am proficient at task and cost-benefit analysis, productivity enhancement, and strategic planning. My most recent achievement was being named Hospital Administrator of the Year. I enjoy the work.

Question: You've never managed a [budget / staff] of this size. What makes you think you can handle it successfully?

Answer: The [budgets / people] that I *have* managed, I've managed extremely well. I have excelled in [strategic use of resources / strategic planning / goal setting / leadership / human resource management]. I have also assisted my manager in the management of her [budget / staff], so in that sense I am experienced. I feel very comfortable that, with my [finance / leadership] abilities, you would be very pleased with my management of the [budget / staff].

Question: You have less experience than our other candidates. Why do you think you are qualified?

Answer: Performance. I am a top performer because of my expertise in [managing the artistic process / sales]. A person could have 30 years' experience and not be able to [mobilize a team to achieve the type of productions that won us the Golden Apple award / sell $20 million in policies].

Question: How do you think your experience in the other [industry / area] qualifies you for this job?

Think about the similarities before you go into the interview. If you are switching departments or industries, this one is sure to come up. Here is an example you can adapt to your industry.

Answer: What is important in your industry is delivering a quality product and building relationships with customers. The same is true in the hotel industry, except our product is tangible (the facility) as well as service. The hotel industry focuses on quality of product and satisfying customers every day. That is what I would be doing for your company every day. As I work to build relationships with your customers, I would capitalize on the communications skills I learned in the numerous training programs Marriott invested in sending me to attend. I would also present your products in such a way that the customer would view us as professional, efficient, and quality driven. I see more similarities and only minor differences.

or

Answer: The similarities are tremendous. Both require careful management to make a profit. Both require flexibility on the part of a manager to adapt to changing schedules and a competitive market. I have achieved outstanding results in both these areas with Delta. I received incentive pay every year for cost management while maintaining excellent quality. I would look forward to bringing that expertise to this job.

Question: Tell me about your years with Acme Company.

Answer: They were gratifying because I was able to accomplish so much. I instituted the first Organizational Development Project. I created the new employee orientation manual, a first for Acme. In every performance appraisal, I was told I met or exceeded all expectations. That led to my promotion to manager.

What if you never accomplished anything and these were terrible years? Think again. Did you get stuck doing anything that was a first for the company? Did you have a meeting or presentation or client relationship that went well? Capitalize on *anything*.

Answer: Those were great years. I learned so much about this industry and particularly about estate planning (substitute your expertise). I built relationships with other departments to improve our department's productivity and turnaround time. I served on key committees, which gave me exposure to the total business and not just our side of the business.

Question: You have so much experience that you appear over-qualified. Won't this be a problem for you?

Answer: On the contrary. I enjoy this work. My experience will make it possible for me to make even greater contributions, and I am a contributor. This is a great position for me to be in.

Answer: I can do this job well, and that is a feeling that will add to my compensation. You know many things contribute to what people consider a good job. I consider this a good job because it capitalizes on my experience. That is a good feeling.

Questions:

1. What experience do you have with [name a strength of yours]?

2. What experience do you have with [name a weakness of yours]?

3. What experience do you have with [name a task that is part of the new job]?

In the questions above, review S.S.S. and PACT in Chapters 2 and 3 to create outstanding answers. Your answers will depend on your particular strengths and weaknesses.

Chapter 20

Questions About
Management

◆

The commerce of the world is conducted by the strong, and usually it operates against the weak.

—Henry Ward Beecher

Are you interviewing for a management position? If so, almost all the questions in previous chapters could be asked in your interview. The following questions, however, are focused on your management style and expertise. Adapt these answers to reflect your approach to management and all you have accomplished so far.

MOTIVATION

Question: Complete this sentence: In managing people, it is important to _____.

Answers: Here are just a few of the acceptable answers:

◆ Communicate well.

◆ Manage people according to their strengths and personality styles.

◆ Identify different strengths and work with individuals to leverage their strengths for their own success and the company's.

◆ Lead them by offering them challenges and opportunities instead of pushing them.

◆ Be their coach and ally in improving performance instead of being totally directive.

◆ Be sensitive to different needs and motivational opportunities.

◆ Give them your vision for where you want the department to go and then allow them to contribute and collaborate with you to make that vision become a reality. Share mutual goals instead of assigning them your goals.

Questions:

1. Explain how you motivate people.

2. What is your primary motivational technique?

Answer: Collaboration. If I can share a vision with someone of how to make his department and his role in it successful, then he will motivate himself. My job is to create an attractive and winsome picture of that vision so that the person wants to be a part of the success. I also need to convey how valuable his skills and contributions are to making that vision a success. People like to feel vital to a company, and successful. Collaboration does that.

or

Answer: I use clarity of goals jointly with attentive follow-up. I find that one is useless without the other. If I have not done a good job of clearly giving the employee a picture of what her goals are, then she is unfocused and less motivated. However, if I give great goals but abandon the employee completely, there is no opportunity for encouragement, support, adjustment, or feedback. Then the employee might not be as successful and become unmotivated.

or

Answer: Self-directed goals with ongoing feedback from me has contributed to my success in the past. I sit down with each staff member and draw a circle that encompasses all we must accomplish—like a big pie. Then I say, "There are four of you. What part of this do you want to be responsible for?" Amazingly, all four get some of what they want.

Then I show them the numbers we must hit by the end of the quarter. I say, "Show me your strategy or schedule of how you want to accomplish this." You know, the schedules they set for themselves are much more aggressive than I would dare set for them.

Along the way, I encourage them and, as a colleague, I keep up with how things are going. I give them feedback and ideas informally and usually I wait to be asked. This method makes them motivate themselves. That is how I have motivated people to achieve such great results, as on the refrigerant management implementation that won the Kirby Award for Best Contribution to the Company. This method also allowed me to increase production without hiring additional people. That's motivation.

CONSENSUS
Questions:

1. Do you believe in managing by consensus?

2. How important is consensus in making tough management decisions?

Answer: Yes, I believe in managing by consensus but I am not hesitant to make a decision if a management decision is needed. Managing by consensus has been highly successful for me as evidenced by my high performance ratings and the improvements in service that led to our earning the Deming Award. Group design of goals means group commitment to goals, and my department and I set the highest goals ever for our group—and we exceeded them. Consensus does not mean, however, abdicating the role of making decisive moves when needed. Sometimes an opportunity presents itself and I need to make a decision. I am also comfortable doing that.

DELEGATION
Question: What is your philosophy about delegation?

Answer: Delegation should be as much for the development of the staff member as it is to redistribute the work. If delegation is done right, the employee has been prepared in some way to be successful in taking on the tasks. This preparation could be by observing, assisting, taking on part of the task little by little, or by formal training. Done right, delegation can get the job accomplished even better and simultaneously develop the employee.

or

Answer: To be successful, a [manager / executive] must delegate. Learning to delegate wisely is something I have learned. There are some tasks that I need to pass on to others and that will broaden their capabilities if I pass it on to them. Delegation is good for everyone.

Question: Are you a strong delegator?

Be careful. Don't appear to be one of those bosses who dumps the worst jobs or problems on his next in line. Yes, you should be a strong delegator, but temper your answer this way:

Answer: I have learned to delegate wisely in my previous jobs. I delegate things to people when they are ready and when it is time for them to take on that responsibility. In that sense, I am a strong delegator. I do not use delegation, though, solely for unpleasant duties or to avoid problems I don't want to deal with.

GOALS/PRODUCTION
Question: How do you set goals?

Answer: By consensus. I get input from everyone on my team; I get the company's input through my boss. Ultimately, I am responsible for creating and clarifying the goals, but everyone becomes a stakeholder in the goals.

Question: How do you determine that your goals are appropriate?

Answer: Since I get collaboration on the front end from my boss and my staff, I know that the goals will be appropriate.

or

Answer: I have never had a problem with this before, so I suppose my method of having all the stakeholders help design the goals is working. I also enjoy ongoing communication with my people, so if anyone were falling short, I would know it and could help.

or

Answer: My employees and management have always rated me highly so that is measurable confirmation that my goals are working for them. More important, look at the results I have achieved: We have increased production by at least 10 percent for three consecutive years. That is even more evidence of goals that work.

Question: What do you do if an employee is not meeting her goals?

Answer: I have not had to deal with this because I have had such great staffs in the past. They went over the top to achieve goals.

If I did have this problem, I would first give the employee the opportunity to solve it herself early on or come to me for help. Then I would begin to communicate with her as a collaborator, a supporter, a teammate. I would offer case studies from my experience and suggestions for changes in strategy. Once I got involved, I would spend time identifying everything that is contributing to the problem. If I could help by reallocating resources or by making adjustments and still meeting departmental goals, I would do that.

Question: What's your track record for [production / results]?

For this, you need to have memorized some accomplishments. Interviewers are more impressed with numbers, revenues, awards with specific names, and dollar amounts.

Answer: Our department produced more widgets in 2007 than had ever come off the line before. At the same time, our quality control improved by 8 percent. I also suggested a method for staffing that allowed us to achieve these results without adding employees. Our company revenues increased by eight million dollars last year and I made a contribution to that.

SALES TRACK RECORD

Answer: I sold more than 80,000 gallons of our leading syrup last year. I personally opened 15 new national accounts. I increased my total number of accounts by 10 percent. My accounts brought in more than ten million dollars in gross revenue. I was the top producer in corporate accounts.

Question: If production is low, explain what you do.

Answer: I've really never had a significant problem with this, so let me think. If I see a temporary dip, I identify causes first to address it strategically. Part of this process is to communicate to the people who report to me. Usually I see the problem resolved at this point.

Occasionally we identify something we need to change in our process or identify a mechanical problem. Most production problems are people issues. I keep in close communication with my people and they are very motivated, so this is not a real problem for me.

INTERPERSONAL

Question: What personal traits do you look for in people when you're hiring?

Answer: I look for an energy and a professionalism that are observed when people talk about their work. If they can tell me with enthusiasm about actual projects or tasks they completed successfully and show that they still have the passion and energy to do that in the future, then I want them on my team. I do look for specifics, however, and not just generalities.

or

Answer: A balance between recent accomplishment and a history of being committed to whatever company they were with at the time. I want to see high performance in recent times, not just old accomplishments. Also, in today's times, we can't expect people to have worked for the same company for 30 years. I do want to see a rationale for the movement from one company to another. I want someone who will contribute to my department before he moves on.

Questions:

1. How would you rate your interpersonal skills?

2. Are your interpersonal skills your strongest asset?

Answer: 10, if you talk to people who work with me every day and to customers. I am a good listener. That opens people up to me and helps me work with people well. I often am the liaison or the catalyst in a department.

or

Answer: My interpersonal skills have been one of the strongest contributors to my success and to my own job satisfaction. My coworkers would rate me 10. I am the "still waters run deep" type. I am a good listener. That is the type of interpersonal skill that many people value. I also learn a lot that way.

EXECUTIVE LEADERSHIP

Question: What has contributed to making you a leader?

Answer: A mix of skills and instincts, supported by a passion for this work. Early on, I developed my management skills by working at Georgia Pacific with some of the best managers in the business. I also took advantage of every training and development opportunity that came my way, and the company invested a lot in young leaders like me. But I think my instincts are by far the most valuable contributor to the success I have enjoyed. I have an intuitive ability to forecast trends and even to detect potential problems before they become problems. I also have good instincts about people, from hiring to handling them in the long term. And I have a high energy level to help me accomplish all I want to accomplish; that helps me perform as a leader.

or

Answer: Insight into people, forecasting skills, receptivity to change and direction, and a love for this industry and my work. I could not

166

have accomplished all I accomplished for Nike if I did not have highly developed perceptivity about people. At the same time, I have always been energized by change and new trends. Whereas some managers in the nineties dreaded changes and innovation, I loved learning about them and fashioning my division to take advantage of innovation and to accomplish even greater things *because* of change and not *despite* it. I think any leader today must have the flexibility and vision to embrace appropriate change.

Question: What has made you ready for greater responsibility?

Answer: Of course, early in my career I did the same preparatory steps others did: earned an MBA, perfected my management skills, became a student of the business, and explored leadership through formal and informal learning experiences. What has really propelled me to this next step is my success in leading others to be successful in one effort right after another. I have had enough success that I know how to take my leadership abilities and apply them to new initiatives. You know about my recent successes in the company such as starting up an on-line marketing branch, but I have translated my leadership to other projects, too. Last year, as United Way chairman, I worked with executives from all the major companies in the city to raise more money than any executive ever has. I am ready to apply this leadership to the position of CFO, and look forward to setting new benchmarks for success in that position.

Questions:

1. What does it take to be a leader?

2. Define leadership.

Answer: Moving people, capital, and ideas forward; setting new benchmarks for progress and then responsibly seeing the progress through by working with every resource identifiable, whether internal or external.

Question: Who is a role model for you as a leader?

You are on your own here. Here is a sample answer.

Answer: Truett Cathy of Chik-Fil-A. He knew how to take appropriate risks and he was a creative thinker. When everyone else was trying to imitate McDonald's success, he was looking for ways to offer consumers an alternative. Although he was strong in cost containment, he was unafraid to charge more because he knew that the high-end quality he pursued would be his market niche. He expanded rapidly, but cautiously, going into places such as shopping malls where at that time he had little competition. He was smart, savvy, and maintained his ethics and standards.

Question: Explain the difference between a leader and a manager.

Answer: Leaders need to be more visionary. They don't just keep up with the market as a good manager must. A leader must forecast and surround himself with the best minds and information in the industry and in business to lead the market—not just follow it. A good leader is partly a futurist and an opportunist on behalf of her company. Although a manager should have vision, she is more compelled to follow through on the vision of the leaders. A good manager, however, will contribute to that vision, and a strong leader will welcome and recognize that contribution.

Question: What is your leadership style?

Answer: Although buzz words abound defining leadership style, I don't think you can pigeonhole mine. That is because I am flexible in adapting my leadership style based on the needs of the organization. Most of the time I am aggressive in the pursuit of improvements, productive innovations, the best talent, and larger market share. But I know when to go into a nurturing state to support my people and resources, much as I did after the recent merger. Today's leader will be more viable if he can glean the best out of each style, assimilate that, and know when to use each style.

VISION

Question: What would you tell a young person starting a career today is the most important thing to do?

Answer: Listen to the very old and the very young. CEOs with years of experience write books and make speeches that are thought-provoking. You can leverage off their experience. But some of the best ideas in art, music, and business have originated in the minds of people under 30. Be open to new ideas. Pursue appropriate risks. Be wise about your career, but be quick to get on board if a new trend starts. Don't resist changes your company has endorsed.

Questions:

1. What do you see is the future of this [industry / profession / department]?

2. What is your vision for [this company / this position / your career]?

Your own version is best here, but you may want to borrow some of the following language.

Answer: My vision for this company is that we would become a leader in the next wave of new products. To do this we need another part of my vision, the best employee pool in the industry.

We would accomplish this by equipping our existing human resources and by making brilliant hires. Our executive team would become scouts and explorers looking for indicators of what the next profitable trends would be. They would look not only for attractive acquisitions but also for creative methods of operating this business using current technologies.

or

Answer: My vision is that we would reinvent ourselves for the rest of the world. We have some great products and outstanding employees. Financially, we look great. But we need to do something to attract the brightest and best leaders and professionals of the future. We should not just be satisfied with our current accomplishments, but make ourselves more exciting and attractive to the market. We are not now known for innovation, but we are the best-equipped company I know to innovate, create, and lead this industry. My vision is that we would devote more energy to projections about the future of this industry and become a powerhouse in what is coming next.

RISK
Questions:

1. Are you a risk taker?

2. What is your philosophy regarding risk?

Answer: Appropriate risk is a necessity, not an option. Being prepared to assess risk is one of the key skills every executive needs to thrive in today's business climate. Most changes bring awesome opportunities to cut costs or create innovative new services. Some changes, however, are not worth the investment of time and

capital. I believe it is my job to make intelligent choices on a timely basis about what risks to take. In the market of the eighties, if I were on the fence about trying something, I would have foregone it. Today, if it were a judgment call I would probably conduct a trial and explore it.

Question: How do you go about assessing and managing risk?

Answer: Although I have incorporated many innovative new philosophies into my leadership style in the last few years, this is one area in which I have a very sound and reliable method that has served me well for many years. I ask myself what all the worst things are that could happen and then I weigh them according to probability and cost. Second, I ask myself what all the profitable things are that could come from this risk. In addition to the bottom line, I envision rewards we might see in our human resources, our leadership in the industry, our image with investors, and our contributions to the community and the environment. I align the two lists. Then I poll all the stakeholders, especially my peers, staff, board members, consultants, and, when appropriate, customers. The answer by that time is usually pretty clear, but I have one more asset to rely on—my instincts. They have propelled me to make decisions such as investing in the new information systems that have saved us their costs many times over. My instincts led me to hire such people as Kathy Harber who, though not from our industry, has been the strongest asset to our corporate staff that we have seen in quite some time. So I believe in appropriate risk as reflected in my successful track record.

Chapter 21

---◆---

Questions About Travel Issues and Schedules

◆

I never travel without my diary. One should always have something sensational to read in the train.

—Oscar Wilde

First, you need to resolve in your own mind how you feel about travel. Don't take a job that requires travel if you can't live with it for a very long time. How much travel can you live with? 50 percent? 20 percent? Realistically, how much travel can your family live with over a long period of time? Know these answers before you interview.

Once you decide what your honest responses are, you can answer the following questions in your own way. These responses are based on the supposition that you have already decided that travel is acceptable to you and your family.

Remember that 50 percent travel may mean Monday and Tuesday some weeks, but Monday through Friday during busy times. Clarify ahead of time if the schedule varies.

ATTITUDE TOWARD TRAVEL
Question: How do you feel about travel?

Answer: I find that I benefit from travel. Although I enjoy my family time tremendously, the time on the road gives me some quiet time to get caught up on paperwork and reading. If I make good use of travel time, I actually have more time on the weekends with my family.

or

Answer: Travel has been such a part of my life that I really don't think of it as a challenge. It is just part of my workday and can actually be pretty interesting. Sometimes the travel gives me additional time to focus on the client I will be meeting and to sort of get into the zone. I really don't understand why some people perceive it as a problem.

Question: Has travel ever been a problem to you?

Answer: No.

Question: How do you deal with travel?

Answer: I have learned to make travel productive and easy. I wear comfortable clothes that travel well, drink extra fluids, and try to get some exercise on the road. I find that I actually get a lot done when I travel. It is really pleasant being away from phones and distractions so I can get some extra reading done.

or

Answer: On my way to a job or meeting, I begin to concentrate intensely on the goals and objectives of the [project / customer]. There is something about being out of the office that seems helpful to this process. The travel time is a great time to go over documents, notes, and other information so I can go into the job or meeting immersed in information about that project.

SALES

Question: Tell me about your experience with [extensive / international] travel.

Specific experiences are impressive. Here is an example.

Answer for Experienced Traveler: I did business for four years in London with Coca-Cola. Later, in my position as marketing director for McDonald's I negotiated the first Paris locations and frequently traveled and worked throughout France and Italy for three years. In 1994 I was traveling more than 50 percent of the time, most of that in Eastern Europe. I enjoy the travel and don't seem to have the trouble some people do with it.

If you have never traveled at all, say as many positive things as you can about your ability to travel.

Answer for Inexperienced Traveler: I enjoy travel. I have the type of stamina that seems to agree with travel and have never experienced jet lag. My favorite cities to visit are Montreal and Mexico City. One thing I find attractive about this job is the travel.

RELOCATION
Questions:

1. How would you feel about relocation?

2. Would relocation be a problem?

Naturally, if you want the job the best answer is that you would not mind relocating anywhere.

Answer: Relocation is not a problem. I have moved for business purposes before and am willing to do it again.

If you can accept relocation, then say so. If you can't, an answer is provided below that is at least diplomatic.

Answer If You Are Opposed to Relocation: Relocation would be difficult for me at this time. We have just moved here to help care for my elderly parents. Although I actually don't have to spend much time in this effort, I need to at least be in the city during this transitional period.

The above answer does not say that you would never under any circumstances consider relocation. You might remain a viable candidate this way. In your answer, use phrases such as "at this time" and "transitional period" to leave the door open.

Question: What are your preferences if we relocate you?

Answer: Naturally, I find your locations in Atlanta and Phoenix attractive, but I am not tied to a location. If you can find the best opportunity for me in this company, I am willing to move pretty much anywhere.

Question: Are there any areas unacceptable to you for relocation?

Of course, the best answer is simply No. If you are really determined, however, to tell an employer you won't go somewhere, give good reasons and try not to sound too inflexible. Don't mention your health or any shortcoming as a reason for not wishing to move. Use some of the same techniques described above. You might try adapting the following answer to your needs.

Answer: Although I am open to many locations, I prefer not to move to an international location until my daughter graduates from high school.

LONG HOURS
Questions:

1. We work long hours during tax season. How do you feel about that? Do you have any conflicts?

2. Because of our global interests, we ask employees to be here at 7:00 A.M. Are you comfortable with that?

3. Working until 9:00 P.M. is not unusual. (SILENCE)

The winning answer is that long hours don't bother you a bit. You knew that. Still, employers today are also concerned about balance, so make sure that you are not viewed as a workaholic—some workaholics don't work as well with teammates who don't share the same work ethic. Also, if you don't care if you get this job or not, this is a great time to negotiate for concessions on hours. In other words, if losing the job won't bother you, you might as well ask for the moon and set boundaries on what you will do and won't do.

Answer: This is work that I enjoy, so long hours don't bother me. I have always worked long hours but I make sure to maintain balance and make time for things that relax me such as kayaking. It works for me.

or

Answer: Long hours seem to be part of this industry; I have come to expect them. Of course, I try to make time for my family and exercise, but working late does not put me off.

This one is risky and to be used only if you don't mind losing this job opportunity.

Answer: Long hours are a reasonable expectation some of the time, especially when there are deadlines. To work long hours every day just to be putting in hours is not the most productive way to work, I believe. I am very focused and work with a high energy level. I use the time at work to its maximum potential. Working that way for 12 to 14 hours a day every day would not be a balanced approach to my work.

WEEKENDS
Questions:

1. This position requires weekend hours. (SILENCE)

2. You will have to work every other weekend. How do you feel about that?

3. Can you be available to work Sundays from 10:00 A.M. until 5:00 P.M.?

Answer If Weekend Work Is Acceptable: I expected weekend hours in this job; it is the nature of our industry. Fortunately, that is not a problem for me.

Answer If Weekend Work Is Unacceptable:

You can probably kiss this job good-bye, but try this.

If there were an unusual circumstance when you needed me to cover for an occasional weekend, I could arrange to do that since this job is very important to me. An ongoing schedule of weekend hours would be difficult for me to commit to at this time. I am enrolled in a weekend degree program and my classes meet pretty much all weekend. If there were any possibility of your working with me on this, I would really appreciate it. In every other way, I feel that this job is a perfect fit.

Chapter 22

Questions That
Show Savvy

◆

Success follows doing what you want to do.
There is no other way to be successful.

—Malcolm Forbes

Are you current about industry trends? Are you a student of the business? Do you keep up? Are you bright, astute, and sophisticated? Do you get the big picture? Are you quick on the uptake? Then you are savvy.

Or, are your ideas about business outmoded and dated? Are you a follower but not an initiator? Are you reactive instead of proactive? Then you lack savvy.

The following questions are ones interviewers use to pick up on how savvy you are. Answering these well can give you an edge when the competition is tight for a job.

GENERAL
Questions:

1. How important is your current job to the overall success of the company?

2. How does your job play a role in your company's strategic plan?

Although this will vary based on your job responsibilities, the following answer will give you a good idea of what works well.

Answer: As the assistant controller for Wellex, my job affects virtually every area of the company. I see this position as being integral to the strategic plan. Because this department is a clearinghouse for the payables and receivables for the entire company, we support and interface with everyone. If we do our job well, we are helpful in making everyone more successful in their roles and in being profitable in this extremely competitive environment. The reporting and analysis we do is critical to projecting where we as a company will invest next. It is this type of responsibility that I am looking forward to.

Question: Did you read *Freakonomics?* (or the current business best-seller)?

Answer: Yes. I especially liked the various global examples. Did you enjoy the book?

or

Answer: No, but it is highly recommended. What did you like about it? After the interviewer responds, be sure to ask if she has read another business best-seller that you actually have read. It is okay not to have read this one book, but don't let her think that you haven't read a business book in years.

Question: If you were sitting here in my place, what do you think you would be asking?

Answer: I would want to know what intangible things I bring to the job, things that might be undiscovered in an interview.

This gives you an opportunity to come up with all sorts of wonderful things about you that may not have been brought up yet.

Question: What interview questions have you used successfully in the past when you were doing the hiring?

Answer: I like the question, "What was an event in your career that stretched you?"

This is a great opportunity to tell about something ingenious that you did, or something that was extremely new and innovative, such as the time you were handed a budget and a contact in New York and were told to make the corporate video even though you had no experience in video. Tell how you hired the director and actors, wrote much of the content yourself, and created a successful video.

INDUSTRY KNOWLEDGE/TRENDS

Question: What trends do you see in our [industry / profession]?

Be prepared for this one. Read up on industry trends before any interview. Your industry has magazines and web sites, some produced by your professional organizations.

Answer: The push in marketing for branding is one trend that interests me. Of course, the company that has done the best job of making their brand highly visible is Coca-Cola. I find it fascinating trying to do similar types of branding for other products. Another trend is the use of on-line marketing. In the last year I have explored this medium and I believe its potential is tremendous.

Question: What are some things you've done to keep your [skills / knowledge] updated?

Answer: I invested in a course in programming, even though I don't do the actual programming. I felt that I could better understand the challenges faced by the programmers if I understood the fundamentals. Another step I have taken is to join the Association of Marketing Executives. There is a great exchange of ideas at the meetings. Speakers keep us aware of future trends and resources we can bring away and apply to our current projects. It has been very productive.

Question: What do you think of the recent move toward deregulation (or any current change in your industry)?

Answer: I think that there are ways to be very successful through the current changes. The keys to thriving for us will be to be willing to innovate and to invest in retraining ourselves.

> **Note:** Always start with a positive.

Question: Are you familiar with the [marketing / operating] techniques of our largest competitors?

Don't fake this one. If you are familiar, mention some techniques and perhaps an example to prove you know your stuff. If you don't, you have learned a very hard lesson about how to prepare for an interview. You may try the following answer, but you may not recover from not knowing something about a company's competition.

Answer: I am not familiar with techniques specific to one competitor. I have educated myself in operating techniques that have been the most effective in the industry such as (insert some techniques).

Question: If you were CEO, what would you be investing in right now?

This is just a disguised way to ask you about industry trends. Use a current trend in an answer like the following.

Answer: As a CEO, I would be very excited about the use of DVD as a way of disseminating training, product updates, and current customer information. I think the potential is tremendous to cut the costs of doing those things as we now do them, yet have better quality and more current information.

FUTURE

Question: How did you hear about this job?

Answer: Another [professional / manager / accountant / technical writer] who is active in the field told me about it.

or

Answer: Martha Heisley, your Director of Marketing, told me about it. She has been very excited about the innovations you are making here and thinks this is a great place to work.

or

Answer: As part of my job search program, I am responding to about a dozen qualified newspaper or on-line ads a month. This position was advertised in the paper.

The last one sounds more professional and well prepared.

Questions:

1. What appealed to you about this job?

2. What are you looking for in a job?

Your sincere answer is best here. You might follow this format.

Answer: Writing and packaging high-tech material is what I do best, and this job provides me with the opportunity to do that every day. Your in-house technical professionals are the best, so writing for them would be a joy. The environment here is very fast paced, and I like that, too.

or

Answer: I want to ally myself with a large, well-respected company like yours. The position allows me to use my talents in graphic design in some really creative ways. This job is what I want on many levels.

or

Answer: I think e-commerce is the next great industry and I want to be a part of it. Your company is on the forefront of this trend. Because I have top skills for this position and you are in the industry I have targeted, the position is extremely appealing.

Questions:

1. What is important to you in a job?

2. What are your priorities in your job search?

Answer: My personal measures of success are most important to me. I have very high standards for my work. This position would allow me to do good work, to innovate, and to make a contribution that would make me successful, all of which are high priorities. Of course, I need the compensation and benefits appropriate to someone at my level in the industry. Finally, allying myself with a leading company like yours is what I am ready for now.

Questions:

1. Ideally, what are you looking for in a company?

2. Describe your ideal job.

Be sure to describe what you can do for the company and not just the ideal schedule.

Answer: The ideal job would provide projects in which I could use my managerial skills, especially my ability to plan work strategically and leverage employee performance. The job would be one in which I knew I could excel yet be challenged by ever-changing projects and tasks. Finally, the job would provide some opportunity for collaboration as well as opportunities to make individual contributions.

Question: How does this job fit into your career plan?

Answer: My entire career has led me to this position. As a career move, this one is exceptional because it capitalizes on all my strengths and experience. From the first job I had as a librarian overseeing a collection of historical papers to my last position as archivist for the *Atlanta Journal*, every experience has honed my skills to make me qualified to lead the development of the Jimmy Carter Library.

Question: Where do you think you'll be in your career in five years?

You must use your judgment here. Some companies want people to show initiative about moving on. Other companies want people who will be satisfied in this position for a while so they don't have a high turnover. Which category does your prospective company fall into? Also, if you know a realistic career path for a successful person in this position, just state it.

Answer: If I am still in this department, I hope it will be because I have been so successful in this position that I have developed it into an even more significant role in the company. I believe that the improvements I can make [to the processing of applications / in quality control / in return on equity / in revenues] will either lead this job to be valued a great deal more or will lead to a [vice presidency / directorship / executive position].

Questions:

1. What goals have you set for yourself short term? Long term?

2. What is your ultimate objective in your career? What part does this job play in that?

This will vary depending on whether you are a nonmanaging professional or a manager. Also, the ultimate goal for a chiropractor will be different from the ultimate goal for a sales professional. Look at what successful people in your field have aspired to. Use their goals to inspire you. Send a message that you are also tops in your field.

Answer: I want to be nationally recognized as one of the top web designers in the industry. That recognition would come from industry awards and professional organizations. My ultimate job would be as the lead designer for a large firm such as yours, or perhaps eventually having my own firm if I ever choose to dilute my efforts by running my own business. At this time, my ultimate objective is to be the best in a corporate setting and not invest in being an entrepreneur.

or

Answer: I aspire to a senior executive position. I plan to open myself up to feedback and development and do whatever it takes to earn a place at the top. I already have the skills, intelligence, work ethic, and initiative. The rest I can learn.

Question: How could you contribute to our company?

> **Note:** Be specific to this position.

Answer: I bring a presentation style to your advertising sales that will be dramatically effective. Not only will my presentations mean greater revenue for the company short term, but the professional standards I set for presentations will raise the bar. I have much I can learn from the staff, and I look forward to sharing my strength.

Chapter 23

The Most Critical Questions: The Ones You Ask the Interviewer

◆

Curiosity is one of the permanent and certain characteristics of a vigorous intellect.

—Samuel Johnson

GOOD QUESTIONS FOR THE INTERVIEWEE TO ASK THE EMPLOYER

In most interviews today, there comes a moment when the interviewer turns to the applicant and asks. "Do you have any questions?"

Do not naively believe that she is trying to be helpful, nor is she concerned about satisfying your curiosity. *This is a test.* I repeat: *This is a test.*

The questions you ask will reveal much to a wise interviewer, such as the following:

◆ how well you have prepared for the interview

◆ your priorities

◆ your values

◆ your level of interest in this job (or lack thereof)

◆ flaws in your work ethic, attitude, or other key traits

◆ your knowledge of the industry and the company

You should take care to ask the very best questions you can prepare. Know for sure that this moment is coming and prepare questions that reflect your intelligence, savvy, and genuine interest in *this* position in *this* company. Following are just a few of the questions you can adapt to your own use.

QUESTIONS THAT MAKE YOU LOOK GOOD

1. What changes would you like to see made over the next year by the person who takes this job?

2. I like customer contact. Roughly, what percentage of the time will I be with customers?

3. Who are your most active clients? Users?

4. Have any changes taken place over the last year that have affected budget, services, staff, or objectives?

   Example:
   You walk into a job that used to offer more customer care, but the budget has been recently cut so you can't give the follow-up your predecessor did. You should find that out now.

5. How much interaction is there with the other departments? Is there good interdepartmental support?

6. Tell me about your top three [clients / training customers / users / people you serve].

7. If you could change one thing about this department, what would that be? If you could add one more resource (human, electronic, or otherwise) to this department, what would that be?

8. Can you give me an example of a project that you felt was successful and tell me a little about what made it successful?

9. We've talked about several responsibilities and goals. What are your top priorities that should be accomplished by the person in this position?

10. If you were sitting here, what would you want to know?

NO-NO QUESTIONS

Don't ask about the following until you have received an offer or strong indication:

◆ vacations

◆ schedules

◆ benefits

◆ time off

◆ type of office

Premature questions about these items make you appear shallow and unsophisticated. You lose the image of being a professional who is interested in what you can contribute to the position. You come off as a short-term thinker, interested only in what you can get from the company.

Naturally, you should address these issues before you sign a contract. In most cases, however, the employer will go over these things when an offer is extended or will put them in a contract for you to read. Do take your time and make sure you are getting what you want. Just don't bring these subjects up too soon.

Chapter 24

Hot Tips for
Finding the
Perfect Job

◆

I might have been born in a hovel, but I determined to travel with the wind and the stars.

—Jacqueline Cochran

Presented here are 40 great tips for acing that upcoming interview. If you have practiced the answers from previous chapters and follow these suggestions, you should come across as a desirable and viable candidate to interviewers.

1. In the interview, sift through what the interviewer says for a nugget about herself. Ask her to tell you more about that particular information. Use caution about exploring personal comments, but follow up on allusions to work, current projects, and so on. For example, if she says she has had a hectic day, ask, "Is this a particularly busy time of the year for your department?" If she mentions she must leave at 4:00 because she is taking a class, say, "I hope it's something interesting." That gives her an opportunity to tell you something about what she is doing, but you are not prying into her personal life.

2. When asked if you have questions, offer a couple of great questions you have prepared (see previous chapter).

3. Prepare some filler statements to buy time. When there is a pause while you consider an answer, say things such as:

   ◆ "How might I best put this?"

   ◆ "Several things come to mind. May I take a moment to give you the one that best applies here?"

4. Create a web site. A web site can package you better than any résumé. The web site can give snippets about your outstanding accomplishments, show pictures of you accepting awards or demonstrating expertise, and even give samples of your work product. Invite the interviewer to visit your web site. Other perks of a web site include

   ◆ Building credibility. You show you use the latest technologies in practical ways.

   ◆ Offering savings on mailings.

   ◆ Intriguing techie interviewers (and there are *lots* of them).

   > **Note:** Earthlink, Office Depot, and college students are great resources for designing your page at a relatively low cost.

5. Memorize a short sentence that answers the question, "What do you do?" For example, "I write business plans and industrial proposals and do seminars."

   You'll need to have this answer ready when people at parties, civic meetings, and church ask you what you're looking for in a job. Since this is the way many of the best jobs are found, make your answer short, clear, and memorable.

6. Things to mention that impress interviewers:

   ◆ You are a lifelong learner.

   ◆ You have your own developmental plan.

   ◆ You support the changes made in your former company.

   ◆ You have done your homework on this company / industry.

◆ You have a career path that shows a logical, upward movement. Even if you take a lower-paying job for a while, you must show that it was for a very good reason: taking courses, moving to a more exciting industry, or starting your own business part time.

7. On your computer, keep the following updated:

◆ your résumé

◆ a project list/portfolio

◆ a one-page flier on your [services / projects / career highlights]

◆ a follow-up form letter

◆ a cover letter

8. Make it easy for the interviewer to get in touch with you through

◆ updated business cards.

◆ an answering machine or service in perfect order.

9. Go on practice interviews. Of course, you don't want to waste anyone's time, but if you think there is a chance that the job might have potential, interview for it. If the job doesn't pay enough, the interviewer may keep you in mind for the next job.

Too many job seekers won't interview unless they are sure that this is the perfect job. If you don't interview for a long period of time, you need to get out there and interview for something. The practice will make you a star in the interview for that really great job—plus, this is a great way to network.

10. Go on informational interviews. These are appointments that you make with contacts to get advice, information, or feedback. You might ask them what industry trends you should be aware of if you are interviewing in their industry. You might ask them for the benefit of their experience if they successfully completed a job search last year.

After an informational interview, you often get a referral. You should close by asking the person to let you know if he hears of opportunities or ask him to mention you to any of his allies in the industry or in his company. Informational interviews often create advocates and allies for you.

11. Practice interviewing with another person. Use the questions from this book.

12. Join a support group or partner with another job seeker during your search.

13. Respond quickly to

- ◆ leads.
- ◆ phone calls.
- ◆ letters.
- ◆ ads.

14. Use vertical marketing. If you are currently employed at a utility, send résumés to other utilities. If you are currently a controller, send résumés to CFOs in desirable companies.

15. Do your research about

- ◆ your industry.
- ◆ this position.
- ◆ your geographic area.

16. Work through professional organizations. For example, if you are a trainer, contact the Job Hotline of the American Society of Training and Development.

17. Divulge intelligently. If you are backed into a corner and must confess to a weakness or mistake, choose something that will make you look like Mother Teresa.

Example:

"I like to contribute. A long training period would be difficult for me. How much of a learning curve do you anticipate?"

Say the above only if you know this company gives minimal training before expecting results.

18. Learn positive negotiation skills. Listen to tapes, go to seminars, or read books. You will probably never be in a better position to negotiate. Learn to get all the perks and bonuses you can without jeopardizing the job.

19. Create a job research space. Designate a workspace or desk devoted to your job search. When you sit there, you know you must get to work in earnest to find that perfect job. Focus your energies and keep your materials in this dedicated spot.

20. Create a schedule and make the job search a [part-time / full-time] job.

21. Get candid feedback from critics as well as friends. Don't ask for a pat on the back. Ask for help working out any kinks.

22. Set behavioral objectives to correct and improve interview performance and find opportunities. Set deadlines for accomplishing changes.

Examples:

◆ Make three cold calls to headhunters by noon each day.

◆ Smile at least three times in each videotaped practice interview: at the beginning, at the end, and at least once more.

23. Invest appropriately in image, services, and résumé. Your interview suit and shoes should be the best you can afford. Your haircut must be current, but not faddish. Your résumé materials should be good quality, but not showy.

24. Drop names cautiously. Don't try to dazzle the interviewer with people you know. He may feel you are playing power games.

You may use names as references. You may even say, "Drew Bentley said to say Hello." Just don't play the name game.

Also, people who work for the same company might not like one another. Dropping the wrong name could hurt, not help.

25. Ask the interviewer one thing from her perspective.

26. Avoid personal and anecdotal comments.

27. Use active listening skills—nod, paraphrase, respond.

28. Network. Network. Network.

29. Explore everything your current employer offers:

- ◆ counseling / advice
- ◆ financing
- ◆ seminars
- ◆ planning

30. Contract. Subcontract. As a contractor for a company, you often get the inside scoop on permanent positions. Or you may be able to see a need, fill it, and invent a position.

31. Develop a polished storefront or exterior image (see #23).

32. Always know the salaries of your coworkers, competitors, and others who do jobs similar to yours. Know what you're worth.

33. Be willing to move.

34. Prepare a stock of noncommittal answers.

Until you have had time to think the situation through, you may not want to toss off an answer you may regret. Still, you want to be perceived as responsive and helpful.

One technique is to agree with any part of what the other person says. Everyone wants agreement. Though you may not agree with the entire message, agree with a portion of it as your starting point.

Example:
If an interviewer were to tell you that his company couldn't pay your required salary because they are not paying the other sales representatives that much, here's how you could answer.

You say, "I agree with your policy of fairness. Being equitable, however, also means rewarding according to achievements and value. I bring to you experience and a pool of new customers. Both of these have value. Companies have traditionally compensated for that value. That is pat of what you will be paying for if you hire a seasoned professional like me."

The responses above may seem painfully obvious, but in a fast exchange of words they have a positive effect.

35. Develop a repertoire of appropriate nonverbal responses.

36. Have a clear understanding of your values.

Know what your spiritual and ethical beliefs are. Write them down. Don't violate these or you will be ineffective.

If you have difficulty defining your values, try this: Ask yourself what you would do if you had only one week to live. That's a good starting point to beginning to define what you value.

You should also resolve what you believe and how you feel about the following:

◆ God

◆ marriage, family, and children

◆ accumulation of wealth

◆ what your definition of success is

◆ charity and giving to the community

◆ your retirement years

◆ death

◆ what material possessions are most important to you

◆ who your best friends are

37. Make a habit of deliberately smiling before answering your phone. You will sound like a personable, confident, energetic employee when potential employers call.

38. Put a broad smile on your face seconds before entering an interview. A little of that smile will still be there despite your nervousness (just in case you forget to smile).

39. Practice good posture. Pretend you are a puppet with a string running up your spine. Use the imaginary string to straighten your back. Don't throw your shoulders back. You will feel uncomfortable and you will look uncomfortable.

40. Practice your handshake with coworkers and friends. Ask if your grip is too loose or too tight. Make sure the skin of the web of your hand (between thumb and index finger) meets the web of the interviewer's hand. Shake the hand of a female interviewer in the same manner that you shake the hand of a male interviewer.

Chapter 25

Before the
Interview: Do
Your Homework

◆

Where observation is concerned, chance favors only the prepared mind.

—Louis Pasteur

Going into an interview prepared is one of the best feelings in the world. Going into an interview unprepared can give you a sick feeling in the pit of your stomach and a bad case of the jitters. Here are the things you can do to assure that you are the most prepared candidate on the day of the interview.

◆ Know the interviewer's name/title and get as much information as possible about him.

◆ Anticipate three questions that you think will probably be asked.

◆ Identify your strengths for this position. Prepare *billboard* answers. A billboard answer is a short but vivid phrase or sentence. (See Chapter 5, page 30). For example:

  – Receiving the National Endowment for the Humanities Fellowship was the highlight of my academic career.

  – Increasing the number of new accounts by 18 percent was part of the reason management promoted me so quickly.

  – Doubling ROI in my first year as a manager was very exciting.

◆ Where are you vulnerable? Prepare short but positive answers to the inevitable questions that will probe your weaknesses.

◆ Practice answers to the standard questions about your experience, education, and past and current jobs.

◆ Research both the industry and the company. Visit the company web site. Look at its brochures and other marketing materials. Read its annual report which is readily available through shareholder relations at a large company.

QUESTIONS TO ASK ALLIES

BEFORE AN INTERVIEW

1. What problems have you faced in the past year? Past weeks?

2. What are some successes? Enjoyable times or projects?

3. What personality type is the decision maker?

4. What could be done better in this position than has been done in the past?

5. What are current goals, tasks, trends, and buzz words?

6. Describe the decision maker. Quirks? Hobbies? Family orientation? Work style? Neat? Disorganized?

7. Any unpleasant experiences or topics to avoid?

8. What is the decision maker's relationship to each staff member? To the boss? To peer departments?

9. What are some things that have gone on in your company in the last year?

10. What are some industry trends?

CONCLUSION

You are now prepared to excel in your interview. No matter what question you face, you have practiced and have some winning ideas for positive responses that will help you showcase your talents, skills, and experience. You have prepared for the interview well. Now you can relax, enjoy the interview as you would any other conversation, and bask in the knowledge that you appear savvy and attractive as a candidate. All you have to do now is say yes when the offer is made!

ABOUT THE AUTHOR

Casey Hawley has conducted seminars on job interviewing for professionals from both sides of the table: interviewees and interviewers. Perhaps that is why her *100+ Winning Answers to the Toughest Interview Questions* offers answers that are so appealing to managers and hiring professionals. She knows what they are looking for because they have been her clients for over a decade.

Ms. Hawley has successfully prepared job seekers applying for positions with Fortune 100 companies as well as start-ups. Her popular seminar titled "Career Change Management" achieves highest ratings for its valuable quick fixes and highly effective techniques for managing the process of securing the perfect job. She is also the author of *100+ Tactics for Office Politics, Effective Letters for Every Occasion, How to Turn Any Employee Into a Star Performer*, and *Living with Your Diabetic Spouse*. Her web site for adult learners, *www.grammarcoach.com*, is considered an innovative approach to helping adult learners upgrade their professionalism through improving their language.

INDEX